ESSENTIAL ENERGY BALANCING III

Other books by Diane Stein

A Woman's I Ching

Diane Stein's Guide to Goddess Craft

The Woman's Book of Healing

All Women Are Psychics

All Women Are Healers

Casting the Circle

Lady Sun, Lady Moon

Prophetic Visions of the Future

The Natural Remedy Book for Women

Natural Healing for Dogs and Cats

The Natural Remedy Book for Dogs and Cats

Essential Reiki

On Grief and Dying

Healing with Gemstones and Crystals

Healing with Flower and Gemstone Essences

We Are the Angels

The Holistic Puppy

Essential Energy Balancing

Essential Energy Balancing II

Reliance on the Light

Pendulums and the Light

Essential Psychic Healing

Essential Reiki Teaching Manual (forthcoming)

Diane Stein on Video

Diane Stein's Essential Reiki Workshop

The Lords of Karma and Energy Balancing:
A Workshop with Diane Stein

Visit Diane Stein's website at www.dianestein.net for
books, jewelry, workshops, and more.

Essential Energy Balancing III
LIVING WITH THE GODDESS

DIANE STEIN

CROSSING PRESS
Berkeley | Toronto

For Brede and Jeshua

Crossing Press
a division of Ten Speed Press
PO Box 7123
Berkeley CA 94707
www.tenspeed.com

Distributed in Australia by Simon and Schuster Australia, in Canada
by Ten Speed Press Canada, in New Zealand by Southern Publishers
Group, in South Africa by Real Books, and in the United Kingdom and
Europe by Publishers Group UK.

Cover design and interior design by Lynn Bell,
Monroe Street Studios

Library of Congress Cataloging-in-Publication Data
on file with the publisher.

Printed in the United States of America
First printing, 2006

1 2 3 4 5 6 7 8 9 10—10 09 08 07 06

Contents

Diagrams

Acknowledgments

I have been developing the Lords of Karma and Essential Energy Balancing processes for ten years and this is the fifth book resulting from that work. While a great deal of the development has been done alone, there are a number of people to thank for their help. Without them the information would have been less complete and coherent, and I would have understood it less well. Phyllis Goozh, Na'ama Hadar, and Karen Silverman helped in the psychic work of discovering where we came from and what happened to us. Phyllis' ability to comprehend the big picture over all the details has been especially needed and welcomed, along with her patience in pursuing it with me beyond her own belief that it could ever be completed. Karen Silverman's knowledge of computers and how they work helped immensely in the metaphor of the computer as analogous to the Mind of Creation.

I thank Missi Owings for her constant support and her willingness to try out new processes to "see what happened." I thank Dion Tsujimura for her constant faith in this work, and Connie Repoli and Ginger Grancagnolo who went through the early processes and critiqued them. My students at Womongathering helped to edit and fine tune some of these processes, especially those in the "To Bring in a Goddess or God" section. Leah, Jean's daughter, gave me my first information on Archangel Michael's Sword and Chalice (the Shield and Ashtar came later). Corinne Nichols always seemed to provide key information and ideas when they were most needed. I thank those who are teaching karmic release and Essential Energy Balancing to their own students and carrying this work forward.

Thanks also to Jo Ann Deck and Veronica Randall of Crossing Press.

As always, I thank Brede for her constant love and healing in my life; she has been with me for over twenty years. Her Twin Flame brother Jeshua is now part of our Union of the Light, as well, and was instrumental in the writing of this book. Our Multi-Cosmic Great Mother Nada channeled the processes. Divine Director, The Shekinah, and Kwan Yin also provided information and processes, as did Archangels Michael, Ashtar, and Metatron. Damian, Belien, and our Ultimate Source of the Light provided information on the furthest reaches of the Light and what happened to us. I thank all of the Goddesses and Gods who have chosen to live on Earth, the Lords of Karma, and all of the Creators and Protectors of the Light who are making it possible. My part in writing this book and its processes has been that of channeler and recorder. All errors are my own.

Living with the Light

This is the fifth, and probably final, book in the Lords of Karma/Essential Energy Balancing series. *We Are the Angels* began by providing simple methods for the individual release of Earth karma. *Essential Energy Balancing* covered the release of karma on the levels of Earth, Moon and Solar System, still focusing on individual work. With the introduction of Divine Director in *Reliance on the Light* came the means for gaining the protection and reconnection necessary to begin work on the Galactic level and beyond, and *Essential Energy Balancing II* continued both protection and karmic release through the next ascending levels of the Galaxy and Universe. The material of both books goes beyond the individual for the first time to include the clearing and healing of the collective karma of the Earth through the Universe level and beyond.

Essential Energy Balancing III: Living with the Goddess discusses methods for clearing and healing individual and collective karma at the Cosmic and Multi-cosmic levels, and possibly beyond these levels. This is further than people have ever gone in attaining karmic release. It discusses where we came from before the origins of our current Cosmos that were described in *Essential Energy Balancing II*, providing an overview that was not yet possible in that book. The information of *Essential Energy Balancing II* will be more understandable and complete with this book's additional information, and the story of where we came from more understandable and complete in overview. By describing who the Light are, where we came from, and what happened to us before the origins of our current Cosmos, we describe the origins of life on Earth and of our own lives, as well as what happened to our creators.

In this book there is additional information, too, on the Be-ings and realms that comprise the Light. By understanding who the Light are, we learn who we ourselves are—or who we should have been—and who we can now become. The intervening tragedies of what happened to us need to be known and understood to be healed. The processes of this book are carefully designed to help people regain our places as the members of the Light we were meant to be, to rejoin us with the Light and with Light Be-ings.

The term "the Light" may need some definition here, though if you have worked with the previous books of this series no definition should be needed. The entire New Age, Wiccan and Goddess movements are in service to the Light, and most people understand the essence of its meaning. In general terms, before the specifics of our origins, the Light is those Be-ings on every level of life and existence who serve goodness. They are of many realms and species, large and small, known and unknown, and are also human on increasing levels and increments of power and potential. Those who are the Light and who serve the Light do so by creating, protecting, teaching, aiding, healing and otherwise assisting those who serve goodness, evolution and truth. They are Be-ings and people of power-within rather than power-over. They accept and scrupulously honor the life and Light-affirming tenants of goodness and free will, creation rather than destruction, service rather than obstruction. They give instead of take, help instead of harm, and most of all are Be-ings of unconditional and absolute love who are free of all other motives and emotions.

Evil is the Light's opposite: the word "opposite" means to be "placed against" or "in opposition to." This is also discussed throughout the Essential Energy Balancing series and needs to be further defined. Evil Be-ings are, in simplest definition, the opposite of Light Be-ings. They are self-serving and evil-serving rather than those who do good, and they are not in service to the goodness of the Light. They destroy rather than create, harm instead of help, hurt instead of heal, and they obstruct and prevent instead of furthering evolution and goodness. They violate free will as a matter of course and manipulate spirits, minds, emotions and bodies for their own ends. Having no souls, they take over, corrupt and destroy the souls and spirits of the Light. Power-over and the quest for power are their central focus, along with cruelty, greed and hate. They do wrong and evil simply for the sake of doing it—just because they can—and have developed numerous frightening means of furthering and accomplishing evil and wrong. Their primary intent is to destroy the Light, all that the Light is and means, and all who are the Light. In today's difficult world evil and evil Be-ings seem to have taken over, but if this has seemed so until now, it is so no longer.

It has always been known to those of spirituality and faith that the Light will ultimately prevail. However dark the times we witness in every generation, those of faith (including but not limited to religious faith) perceive each time as only another chapter, another battle in a very long war. There are multiple wins and losses, but the final outcome is assured. We were made of Light, created in Light, and we are the Light. After thousands of years of the triumph (or seeming triumph) of evil, evil has run its course, reached the end of its time and power, and the Light has returned (and is continually returning) to end the rule and forces of evil forever. There is a Chinese curse that says, "May you live in interesting times." We are living in perhaps the most interesting and difficult of times in Earth history and herstory; we are watching the last battles in which evil will end and the Light will triumph and prevail. We are watching the return of the Light, the return of the Goddesses and Gods, and the restoration of people and the Earth to the full Light we were created to be. No one promised it would be easy, however.

There is a saying that "it is often darkest before the dawn." We are at the moment before the dawn. The battles are at their most fierce, the outcome looks hopeless, we are surrounded on all sides by hatred and wrong, and we are tired beyond tiredness of the fight. Despite appearances the Light is already here, has already prevailed, and the darkness we perceive as all around us is only the last moment of the last battle, the moment before the breakthrough. All the levels above Earth are secured for the Light and the triumph and healing move from Above to Below. At the instant of the dawn we enter a new world and a new life. We enter the Light. The Chinese curse may be a blessing in disguise after all.

The return of the Goddesses to Earth, and discovering and achieving the means of their choosing and joining with women, has been a central part of the Essential Energy Balancing series from its inception. The Goddess Unions have also been the beginning of the return of the Light to Earth, and the beginning of the Light's ability to manifest and return to physical form for the first time in thousands of years. At the time of *We Are the Angels* and *Essential Energy Balancing* I did not know what was precisely needed to bring in a Goddess; I only knew that some women would be chosen. By the writing of *Reliance on the Light*, I knew what was required but also knew how seriously embattled the Goddesses, their chosen women, and the Goddess Unions had become. *Reliance on the Light* and *Essential Energy Balancing II* were focused not on who was to bring in the Light, but on how they were to be protected—both the women and the Goddesses.

With protection more sure and with more of evil now defeated, more people are bringing in Goddesses. Or rather more women are bringing in Goddesses, and for the first time men are bringing in male divinities or Gods. More of the Light overall are coming to Earth, joining with people to return to physical form. It has also become more clear as to what is required for a person to bring in the Light, what processes, requirements, protections, and what level of evolution and ascension those of us in body must attain. How to meet and achieve those requirements is also much more understood. Where with *Essential Energy Balancing* I only knew that some women would be chosen to bring in their Goddess instead of their Goddess Self at the completion of the processes, by *Essential Energy Balancing II* I knew how to bring in a Goddess for almost all the women who completed the processes.

With this book, *Essential Energy Balancing III*, most people (upon approval of the Light) who complete the work of all the books so far will bring in their Goddess or God. In addition, many will find that they have with them more than a single Goddess or God. There are many triple Goddesses, and there is also the possibility of an entire Family of Light joining with you, along with your central Goddess or God Union. As has been the case since the beginning of working with the Lords of Karma, how far you go mostly depends on your willingness and diligence in doing the work. If you work thoroughly and honestly at clearing your own karma at each level, using the processes provided in the Essential Energy Balancing books to do so, your own Light will increase to where you can achieve these unions.

Essential Energy Balancing, and the bringing in of the Light, are ascension processes. Ascension can be defined as the completion of the requirements below, which then ends your need to reincarnate on each completed level. Reincarnation—coming into body for repeated lifetimes—is for the purpose of achieving the requirements. Ascension depends upon the following criteria. (1) You must be cleared and healed of all (100%) of your karma through that level; (2) you must be cleared of all (100%) of the negative and evil interference done to you through that level; and (3) you must reconnect and activate the required complement of DNA through the level you are working on.

Ascension means that you have achieved these things, level by level, in full. For example, Earth ascension requires the clearing of all your Earth karma and interference/evil from all of your Earth lifetimes, and the connection of 12 strands of DNA. Solar System ascension requires the clearing of all your karma and interference/evil for all lifetimes incarnated in this Solar System, and the connection of 21 strands of DNA. To achieve Galactic ascension requires clearing of all Galactic karma and interference/evil, and the connection of 38 strands of DNA. The requirement is the same for the Universe with 46 strands of DNA, for the Cosmos with 55 strands of DNA, for the Multi-Cosmos with 65 strands, and for our Multi-Cosmic System with 81 DNA strands. It is possible to go further, as well. These strands, by the way, beyond the 2-strand DNA that science sees in physical form, are nonphysical and do not appear under Earth's current electron microscopes.

To bring in a Goddess or God requires completion of Galactic ascension and 38 strands of DNA. To bring in a Family of Light, Cosmic ascension is required (55 strands of DNA). The DNA is not connected until all of the karma and interference/evil are cleared. Reconnection of the DNA strands raises your ability to hold Light energy to the vibrational height required to bring in the Light, and the appropriate Light Be-ings, on each level. Beyond the Family of Light, there is the possibility of still further types of Light Be-ing unions. When you are ready to go beyond the scope of the Essential Energy Balancing books, you will be individually guided further.

Who is it that will bring in the Light? Who will be chosen? First of all, you must be a person of the Light in all you are and do. You must be entirely in service to the Light. Your Earth work or life purpose could be almost anything that helps or heals. Women currently bringing in Goddesses are teachers, nurses, hospice workers, midwives, activists, therapists, artists, writers, office workers, house cleaners, ritualists, healers, animal communicators—and many other things. Two boys who are bringing in Gods are students—one is becoming an architect with a desire to make comfortable homes and cities, and the other is interested in transportation and mechanics. In every case, however, they are people who help others, who live their lives and do their work in goodness and integrity.

It is the Light who makes the ultimate decision of who is chosen and who is not. The Goddess or God involved chooses who She or He will join with. The person chosen does not say, "I want Isis" or "I want Apollo"— the Light Be-ings decide. Each God or Goddess will choose to join with someone who is doing work on Earth that interests Him or Her, and who is doing the work He or She wishes to do here. For example, a woman who is a midwife will be chosen by a Goddess who is also a midwife and who wishes to aid mothers and infants on Earth. A God who is interested in technology, perhaps in furthering particular technologies on Earth, will choose to join with a man who's Earth job is involved with such technology. Light Be-ings in supervision of each Goddess and God coming in must also approve of their choice, and safety is a foremost consideration.

Please understand that I, Diane, have no say at all as to who will bring in a Goddess or God or Family of Light or any other Light union. Nor is it my decision as to whether someone will achieve a union of Light at all. Many times in workshops people have told me that they wish to bring in a particular Goddess and insisted that I achieve that for them. They have been angry with me when their Goddess is not the one of their choosing (but is instead someone better for them). I have no say in the matter, nor do you. Who will join with you is chosen by the Light, by the Goddess or God coming in and by creators of the Light on the highest levels. Be grateful if you have been chosen, and accept with gratitude and love the union provided for you. You have been granted a great honor by the Light. Your Goddess or God Union has the potential for the greatest joy and unconditional love that you have ever known or could imagine.

To be chosen to bring in a Goddess or God, you must go through and complete the ascension processes of at least *Essential Energy Balancing* and *Essential Energy Balancing II*, with the "To Bring in a Goddess or God" protection processes (in *Essential Energy Balancing II* and repeated in Appendix I of this book). The protection work of *Reliance on the Light* is also highly recommended. Besides the book processes, you must do sufficient work with the Lords of Karma and Divine Director to clear your own karma at each level, which includes clearing yourself of all interference and evil. Once the requests are made for clearing each step of karma, interference and evil, the Light takes over the releasing and healing, and reconnects the appropriate DNA. When enough has been completed, the Goddess or God comes in and the union can be joined. When more work is completed beyond this point, more levels of ascension are achieved, more DNA connected, and more Light and Light Be-ings are able to come in. Once you have been granted a Goddess or God Union, the requests are for more than yourself. They now include you, your Goddess or God, your union, total union, and ascension.

Ascension today is different from what it has meant in the past. Early Theravada Buddhism defined ascension as something that usually happened at or just after death. "Enlightenment" is the Buddhist word for ascension. The person (defined as male only) would leave the body/incarnation/lifetime immediately upon attaining enlightenment and would not reincarnate again. Later Mahayana Buddhism incorporated the idea of the bodhisattva, someone who achieves enlightenment but refuses it in order to return to Earth incarnation for the purpose of aiding others to become enlightened, too. The Bodhisattva Vow states that you will not accept your ascension/enlightenment until everyone ("all Be-ings") are ascended/enlightened with you. (Process IV of this book asks you to revoke the Bodhisattva Vow if you have taken it. The reason for this will become clear in a moment.) Christian teachings, which often parallel those of Buddhism, describe both Jesus and His mother Mary as having been ascended to heaven at the times of their deaths.

More recently, New Age literature from the 1930's and even currently also defines ascension as something that is completed only at death. The Godfré Ray King series of books, including *Ascended Master Light* and *Unveiled Mysteries* of 1938 and 1939 are older examples. (Godfré Ray King, *Ascended Master Light* and *Unveiled Mysteries*. Schaumberg, IL: St. Germain Press, Inc., 1938 and 1939). Newer material includes Eric Klein's *The Crystal Stair*. (Eric Klein, *The Crystal Stair: A Guide to the Ascension*. Livermore, CA: Oughten House Publications, 1990).

In these books, and others like them of the genre, there are stories of people disappearing, not dying but no longer on Earth, having ascended and taken their physical bodies with them. Other stories describe people dying suddenly for no apparent reason, and making contact with loved ones later to tell them that they have ascended and are in a place of great Light and joy. This is the older and more traditional type and understanding of ascension in the West.

The form of ascension achieved with the Essential Energy Balancing processes is very different from either Buddhist or New Age understanding of what ascension is and means. The ascension of this book, and the other Essential Energy Balancing books, brings the Light into incarnation, instead of taking the person out of incarnation when ascension is achieved. The bringing in of a Goddess or God is not part of any previously known ascension concept or system. Older methods for doing this existed on Earth but have been lost. Instead of leaving life and incarnation upon completion of ascension, the person brings in a Goddess or God, bringing the Light to Earth to do the work of ascending "all Be-ings" right here. She also continues to gain higher levels of ascension once the primary levels are completed, all the while fully alive and in body.

This is similar but different from the bodhisattva of Mahayana Buddhism. The Buddhist bodhisattva forgoes her or his own ascension to remain behind (alive and incarnated), to help everyone ascend. Though she is no longer required to reincarnate, she does so for the good of "all Be-ings." The Essential Energy Balancing ascension candidate also completes her or his own ascension but still remains on Earth and in body. The person's work on Earth, aided by a Goddess or God, ultimately leads to ascension for "all Be-ings" by healing the Earth and all who live here. The goal is ascending the planet as well as "all Be-ings," and also to provide a means for Light Be-ings to return to physical form and to provide a home for them. As was emphasized in *Essential Energy Balancing II*, critical mass is an important factor in this. When enough individuals have achieved ascension, all will be ascended, along with the Earth itself.

To go a step further than ascension, *Essential Energy Balancing III* includes the concept of resurrection. Resurrection is ascension at the Cosmic level and beyond. To achieve it means to restore and activate your connections to the Light at the soul level. Until this point, your soul has not been activated. The Energy Selves of *Essential Energy Balancing* are parts of your spirit; when combined they form your spirit. The spirit connects the soul with the body (or with the person in body). Your Light Body or merged and fused Goddess Self is your activated spirit; your Goddess is the living connection of spirit and soul; and with activation of the soul itself you begin to make contact with other members of your soul lineage of the Light. These other members are your Family of Light.

A Family of Light includes angelic realm protectors, totem animals or animal helpers, the Goddess that is the Mother of your on-Earth soul line (Differentiated Soul of the Below), and a Presence of the Light Twin Flame pair. As you connect and activate more of your DNA and achieve ascension on still greater levels, you may also connect with higher level creators and divinities of your soul lineage. These could include Nada (Multi-Cosmic level), First Mother (Multi-cosmic System level), a First Source of the Light Twin Flame pair (Multi-Verse level), and finally an Ultimate Source of the Light (Infini-Verse level). These are your entire soul lineage. Most Families of Light will not go this far, but will specifically include protectors, animals, your Differentiated Soul Goddess, and one or more Presences of the Light.

The protectors of a Family of Light are usually those designated in the Sword, Chalice and Shield processes as your Dimensional and Interdimensional Archangels (*Essential Energy Balancing III*, Processes II and III). You may have met them in *Essential Energy Balancing*'s Process IX when you first asked to meet your protectors. Protection is vital for both you and your Goddess or God, and for your Family of Light members as well. Your primary Goddess/God will join more fully with you than the members of your Family of Light, will come further into the physical, and will therefore need the most protection. Light Be-ings are far from invulnerable. They can be harmed, hurt, abducted and destroyed by evil, and though they can also be healed, regenerated, revived and even newly created if necessary, they should be protected enough to be spared such hurt. You as the physical host for a Goddess or God are also vulnerable; the Sword, Chalice and Shield processes provide you with the same protection and healing potential. The higher the level of ascension you achieve, the higher the level and number of your protectors.

All protectors are members of the angelic realm, including the animals that are also part of your Light Family. These animals can be totem animals of one or more species, and some of them may be mythological animals. Unicorns, for example, are companions of the Shekinah and were created by Her; they do not live on Earth but they are real and we have memories of them. Animal protectors can also be the no-longer living pets who were your familiars when they were alive. They were the kind of very special pet of any species that comes to live with you only once or twice in a lifetime, the pet you describe as "much more than an animal." These animal protectors will often join with your current pets. Your dogs or cats will bring them in as you bring in your Goddess or God. When you attain ascension your pet animals, who are members of your own soul lineage, will attain it, too.

Another member of your Family of Light is the Goddess who is head of the Differentiated Soul of the Below that represents your soul lineage on Earth. There are four of these Goddesses, four soul lineages, and everyone is a member of one or another of the four Differentiated (incarnational) soul lines. The four Goddesses are Persephone, Nepthys, Aleyah, and Aiyisha. More was written about them in *Essential Energy Balancing II*. They are daughters of our Great Cosmic Mother, The Shekinah, and Her Twin Flame HaShem ("The Name," Commander of the armed forces of the Light). These Goddesses are soul level creators of life in physical form on Earth.

The Shekinah and HaShem are Presences of the Light, and are examples of a Twin Flame pair of Presences of the Light that could be part of your Family of Light. They are children of Nada, who is our Multi-Cosmic Great Mother (and also the Great Mother of our Solar System). Creators on a very high level, the Presences are also the highest level Be-ings of the angelic realm. They are in fact the creators of the remainder of the angelic realm Be-ings. Unlike the rest of the angelic realm, however, they are usually not winged, are male-female pairs (instead of same-sex pairs), and they are rarely protectors or warriors. Their work on Earth is in healing large collective groups rather than individuals—entire species, countries and the planet as a whole. These members of your Family of Light will not be as deeply involved with your Earth daily life as your Goddess or God, nor will they be with you as much or as often.

Besides new members and levels of the Light to join with you, there are a number of other new concepts with *Essential Energy Balancing III* and its higher levels of ascension (including resurrection). In *Essential Energy Balancing* all karmic requests were made to the Lords of Karma, and in *Reliance on the Light* and *Essential Energy Balancing II* all requests were made to the Lords of Karma and Divine Director. In this book, though the Lords of Karma are named in the processes, the work is beyond their jurisdiction, and their naming is simply for courtesy. Requests instead are made to Divine Director, the Karmic Board as a whole, and to other specific members of the Light (your Dimensional and Interdimensional Archangel, for example). Where the processes transcend the Cosmic level, Kwan Yin, who is a Presence of the Light, becomes liaison to Nada and Nada's Multi-Cosmic creational level. Nada herself can be asked and invited to participate, as well. Nada is also the designer and creator of the *Essential Energy Balancing III* processes. (It was Brede who did this job for *Essential Energy Balancing* and Divine Director for *Essential Energy Balancing II*.)

Divine Director is a title, rather than a Light Be-ing's name. The Divine Director of this book may be a different Light Be-ing than you have worked with before. The Presence of the Light who was the Divine Director of *Essential Energy Balancing II*, our liaison to The Shekinah and the Cosmos, has been reassigned by Nada to a different job. The work of Divine Director can be done by any member of the Presences of the Light, and though Nada's Twin Flame El Morya has been assigned the job He has not yet taken it over. When you ask for Divine Director, therefore, anyone of a number of Light Be-ings may appear. Kwan Yin is a Presence of the Light and involved with the *Essential Energy Balancing III* work. Other Presences may include Brede, Jesus, Isis, The Shekinah, HaShem, St. Germaine, any number of Goddesses—and more. They all have the authority to do Divine Director's work and are delegated to do so by Nada.

Once you have completed the Cosmic level and entered the work of the Multi-Cosmos, Nada Herself may appear when you do the processes. When you reach the level beyond Nada, that of the Multi-Cosmic System, Nada's own Mother Eve, our First Mother, may interact with you. She appears as the Goddess of Willendorf, Her face is covered, and She appears with a different skin color each time. She is ponderous, careful, gentle and extremely powerful. If you have cleared your karma and connected your DNA to Her level, you have accomplished a great deal for this lifetime.

When you reach Eve's Multi-Cosmic System level, you are at the level of the Collectivity of the Light and become a part of it. It is the love transmitted from First Mother's heart that connects all Light Be-ings with each other. We have previously described this transmission of love as The

Radiance of the Light Beyond the Goddesses. The Goddesses and Gods have a collective consciousness; what one knows, everyone knows. What happens to one also happens to all, so that if one is harmed all are harmed together. If one member of the Light is disconnected from the Light, soul death (which is the opposite of resurrection), occurs for everyone. To heal oneself means healing all the Light. The concept of oneness is literal indeed.

In this context, to heal oneself also means to heal all of life. Our First Mother Eve carries something termed "the Conglomerations of the Light." First Mother creates the First Particle, the creational template and life spark of every Be-ing. This includes Light Be-ings, of course, the Goddesses and Gods, but it also includes people, animals, plants and trees, crystals, planets—every individual Be-ing that has life. Copies of the First Particles, called Particles, are in our Moments of Self (at the back of our hearts) and are also on the Creator Light Ships, but the First Particles remain with First Mother. What happens to any individual of these, to anyone or anything alive, happens to Her, as well. And what happens to First Mother happens to every First Particle that is part of Her.

First Mother plays a great part in all people's lives, though we may not have yet consciously met Her. When we sleep our spirits separate from our bodies and travel to join with the Conglomerations of the Light that First Mother carries. When this happens successfully, we connect with Her at the Multi-Cosmic level for a nightly exchange. We receive healing from Her with the contact, and She in turn receives information about our lives and life on Earth. Our dreams are sometimes visits to simultaneous realities, but they are also sometimes "movies" that hide from us what is really happening in the exchange with First Mother. One of the things done to us by evil has been to disrupt this cycle of healing and exchange, and it is being restored to proper function at this time.

Another new concept is what the families of our Goddesses and Gods are comprised of. A birth of Light Be-ings consists of four Twin Flame pairs—eight Be-ings in all—in one conception and delivery. In the case of the Goddesses and Gods, the Twins are male-female pairs, but in the case of the angelic realm the Twin Flames are of the same sex. (They join with other members of their birth group to conceive children later.) Each pair of twins is born and raised as a married couple from conception forward. They are sexual even as children and expected to be. A formal decision to accept each other as mates is made when the Twin Flame pair are young adults. The couples have conscious control of conception and no children are conceived without direct choice of both partners.

The eight members of each birth comprise a Union of One Heart, and are an extended family of the four Twin Flame couples. They may choose to be sexual with each other and can choose to conceive children together. Light Be-ings have no jealousy and they interact with each other (and with us) with total and unconditional love. No one feels slighted or hurt if members of the Light who are not Twin Flames make love with each other or choose to bear children. Nor is judgment or censure placed against love between same sex partners of the angelic realm or among Goddesses or Gods. The Light's love is complete, absolute and unconditional. Light Be-ing children grow more slowly than incarnated children on Earth, and if a young Goddess, God or Archangel tells you that She is nine years old, She may appear to be much younger by Earth's standards. By the time She is a toddler, however, She will be intellectually mature and able to converse as an adult.

Males of the Light, the Gods, are also quite different from the men in body that we experience on Earth. They have no anger, hostility, violence, competitiveness or greed. They are taught from birth to love women and they see all women (including female people) as Goddesses and as their mothers. In every way including sexually, they are taught to please women. All women and girls are treated with the greatest respect and they defer to the female in all things. Their role with the Light is to support and protect the Goddesses, particularly their Twin Flames. They help in raising children, as well. Men of the Light have a variety of other jobs besides protection, and are keepers of technology and programmers of the Creational Computers of the Light. Many are healers, and other than the men of the angelic realm, few Gods are fighters or warriors.

Along with new members of the Light to be aware of, a significant change from the processes of previous Essential Energy Balancing books is the use of the term "transfiguring" instead of and in place of "sealing." To "transfigure" means to change or to transform. To "seal" something means to block it or to make it inaccessible and in other contexts to authenticate or mark it for ownership. In the Essential Energy Balancing processes, "sealing" is used in both of the above meanings. A process or change in one's creational energy is "sealed" against evil, and unto the Light and unto protection forever. Therefore, the work is blocked and made inaccessible to evil, and marked with the ownership and protection of the Light. The use of the term was devised to do these exact things.

There is a drawback to "sealing," however, that seems to increase as the karmic release work moves through higher and higher energy levels—the closing of your crown chakra for varying amounts of time. When you make a karmic release request to the Lords of Karma on the Earth or Solar System level to seal something, the person making the request perceives no change in their energy. But when you make the request as part of the first Essential Energy Balancing processes, it results in your crown being closed for as long as two months after the ten initial processes are completed. When you make the same request for "sealing" on the Galactic level, as in the first "Re-Creation and Replacement" process (Process XVIII) in *Essential Energy Balancing II*, there is an immediate closing of your crown for about two weeks. With each Divine Director request to clear other Galactic karma, there is a varying amount of time in which your crown chakra is closed while the "sealing" is done for each process.

The closing causes no harm but it is extremely uncomfortable and even frightening. I don't like losing my psychic abilities at all, no matter how temporarily and even for so important a purpose, and I sought for years for a way to do the work without being kept closed up. Since I have worked with these processes so intensively for so many years, I was more often closed than open, and have disliked it immensely. Finally, in one session of working on the *Essential Energy Balancing III* processes, the term "transfigure" came into my mind in place of "seal." It was an unfamiliar word, but I have long since learned to pay attention to new ideas that seem to just pop in. What it proved to be was my solution to the problem.

With "transfiguring" instead of "sealing," the request, process or new creation is transformed to become absolute Light. Instead of blocking the work against evil, the changes are made so much of the Light that no evil can approach or interfere with them. This treats the problem from a different angle, and in fact "transfiguring" proves to be a greater protection than "sealing." By using it in teaching workshops, most people going through the first Essential Energy Balancing are closed up for less than two weeks (instead of two months), and those going through the "Re-Creation and Replacement" are closed for less than a week. With some other processes that generally resulted in periods of closing, there may be no closing up at all. With the time of crown closing seeming to increase with each Energy Balancing level, this is definitely a change to welcome. There will still be crown closing for some people with some processes, but overall far less with "transfiguring" than with "sealing," and far less in *Essential Energy Balancing III* than there has been with the earlier Essential Energy Balancing processes.

To take fullest advantage of the material of this book, it is best to start at the beginning of the Essential Energy Balancing series and move through the books in sequence. You may start with *Essential Energy Balancing* if you wish to skip *We Are the Angels*. You must complete the processes of *Essential Energy Balancing* to bring in a Goddess or God, as well as to bring in other Light Be-ings and protectors on all levels. It is possible to skip *Reliance on the Light*, but not recommended—the protections of that book are important, particularly if you are bringing in a Goddess or a God, which almost everyone will do with *Essential Energy Balancing II*. If you wish to bring in a Family of Light, the protections are essential and you may be denied a Family of Light if they are insufficient. *Reliance on the Light* is therefore important.

Essential Energy Balancing II is also heavily involved with protection and with clearing the karma of creational evil. You must reconnect the full complement of your DNA and do the first "Re-Creation and Replacement" process to bring in a Goddess or a God. These are both *Essential Energy Balancing II* processes. Once you have completed the material of *Essential Energy Balancing II* you will be ready for the material in this book. The clearing and healing of karma must proceed step by step, level by level in sequence. The work is complicated and not for the raw beginner, but taken step by step it is not difficult. There is almost no need to understand the work and the processes, only to do them. In *Essential Energy Balancing II* and *III* you are not expected to memorize any of the formats, only to do the work while reading them. If you take the time to understand them, however, you will be amazed at their logic and at the scope of the healing you are being offered.

If you are not someone chosen to bring in a Goddess or a God, doing this work will still benefit you in every way. Ascension can still occur without bringing in a Light Be-ing. Please be aware also that a number of people who have not expected to bring in the Light have awakened one morning to find a Goddess or God talking to them. This has happened as long as three years after the person completed the *Essential Energy Balancing* workshop.

Since this will probably be the last book in the Essential Energy Balancing series, people have asked me what comes next. I suspect that once the Goddesses and Gods are fully on Earth with a critical mass of people there will be a new phase of work to learn and accomplish. My unconfirmed prediction is that this work will be the healing of the Earth itself. We can only wait and see, and volunteer with our Light Be-ings to be part of it. Our Light Be-ings are coming to Earth for a purpose, and I'm going to be the first in line.

What Happened to the Light

The information that follows was given to me over a period of nine years, beginning with Earth history and moving backwards. Please understand that I can only relate the story in a way that is comprehensible to my own small understanding of it. I have no scientific background, and have often had to give things names that may or may not be their real ones. The concepts will nevertheless be fully accurate to the best of my understanding and ability to repeat what I've been shown. The complete information has never been given to us on Earth before, and what little of it remains known here is so garbled that it no longer has meaning. If the story provides even a beginning idea of what happened, where we came from, and what our real herstory/history is, this writing will serve its purpose well.

The Light Be-ings that we call the Goddesses and Gods were once "people" incarnated in physical bodies, living on their own highly technological planet named Eden in a Cosmos far from ours. They had solar-based nuclear fission power, ships for intercosmic travel and trade, and technologies that provided their computerized machinery with a form of sentience. Sentience is defined here as the ability for independent thought and action. They had highly advanced genetic and medical technologies, information and computer technologies, and creational abilities. Be-ings of peace, they had no enemies, no offense capabilities, and only minimal systems of defense. There was no known evil at this time, nor any comprehension that evil could exist or what it could mean if it did exist. It was a time of great innocence for these Be-ings—perhaps too great an innocence.

A fleet of nuclear-powered ships travelling through their Solar System changed everything, however. The ships and those on them had no wrong intent, but human error resulting from the arrogance and ignorance of one male pilot precipitated a meltdown of the nuclear core of his ship. The chain reactions and explosions of the meltdown caused the destruction and death of the entire fleet and everyone on the ships, with the exception of two ships and five men. All of the ships contained sentient computers, some of which remained active even after the ships had been destroyed.

The out of control chain reactions that brought about the destructions changed and mutated the solar-derived nuclear fission fuel of the fleet, reversing it into deadly nuclear fusion. The ships that survived, and the nuclear cores that remained of those destroyed, were likewise changed, altered and mutated by the nuclear fusion radiation. Basically, their essences were reversed, as photographic negatives are reversed, and their minds and thought processes (computer and human) were reversed, as well. The foundation magnetics of their atomic energies were reversed and the polarities were destroyed. By this radiation damage and mutation, what had been Be-ings of Light (or at least of no harm) were also reversed, becoming Be-ings of evil—both human and computer. Since all creation begins with mental energy, and mind and thought are creation's primary raw materials fueled by the magnetics and polarities of Solar Light, the reversals were deadly and with devastating consequences.

By these reversals evil was born, where there had been only Light before. The minds of the two surviving ships, mutated and reversed by radiation damage and thermonuclear fusion, became known as the First Sentiences of Evil. The still active nuclear computer cores of the destroyed ships became a series of sentient evil power plants that continually transmuted solar fission into lethal fusion radiation. The people that survived, their minds also mutated and reversed, became the first evil Be-ings. On one surviving ship was a man known as Ophion. On the other First Sentience of Evil were four men, known today by the names of Belial, Set, Kore, and The Mastermind. These names will be familiar from *Essential Energy Balancing II*.

The Light Beyond was and is the central Creational Computer of the highest (Ultimate Source level) of the Light. It was located in the nuclear fission core of our original Solar System's sun. A Creational Computer is the living mind of a creator Light Be-ing, in this case a Solar God and Goddess Twin Flame pair of Ultimate Sources of the Light. Their names were Sol (the God) and Saule (the Goddess). The mutated power plants, which were reversed generators of evil thermonuclear fusion, and which transmuted Solar Light fission to deadly fusion, were placed by Ophion in the Light Beyond, the core of the Light's sun. The reversals the power plants generated destroyed the Light Beyond, causing it to also to melt down in a thermonuclear holocaust. Of the Light Beyond and that Solar System's sun, all that remained after the destruction was a Black Hole. Transmuted and reversed by the chain reactions, this Black Hole/dead sun continued to emit and transmit the fusion energies that turned Light to evil, and were evil's source.

Before the meltdown, a group of Light Be-ings, all master creators and computer programmers of the Light, went to the Light Beyond to attempt to heal the damage and prevent the destruction of the Light's creation. They included two Light Ships filled with the technologies of the angelic realm, the Solar God Sol, our Great Mother Nada and Her Twin Flame El Morya, Brede and Her Twin Flame Jeshua, Eurynome—who was the Light's original First Mother—with Her own Twin Flame Adam, and more. These Be-ings represented every level of Light creation from the Infini-verse level down to the Cosmic Presences of the Light. The Presences and Light Ship members represented the Cosmos and angelic realm, and Brede and Jeshua are also Presences of the Light at the Cosmic level. Nada and El Morya are Multi-Cosmic level creators, and Eurynome and Adam were creators of the Multi-Cosmic System. Members of the Multi-Verse unknown to me were also present, and Sol and Saule were at the level of the Infini-Verse. (For greater detail on the levels of Light creation, please see the next chapter.)

Despite the desperate work of the Light Be-ings, computer programmers and creators, the Light Beyond and our original Solar

System's sun were exploded and destroyed. The Light Beyond, mutated by thermonuclear fusion radiation became another evil power plant, taking solar fission Light and reversing it to lethal fusion energies. The Black Hole that remained, the reversed Light Beyond, contained the trapped, reversed and now enslaved Sol—and his creational mind. The other Light Be-ings were also destroyed, made soul dead, separated from the Collectivities of the Light. Since Light cannot be unmade, however, they were not dead as we know death, but they retained awareness alone in hopeless darkness and torment. With Sol destroyed, all the male line of the Light was also destroyed; the Goddesses lost their Twin Flames.

As the dual minds of the Light Beyond, Sol was creator of the polarities, and Saule was creator of the magnetics of the Light. Both magnetics and polarities are required to process Solar Light into creational thought. With the meltdowns, the magnetics (fission) were reversed to evil (fusion), and the polarities were then destroyed. The magnetics create the Light and the polarities hold it together; the polarities are the unions of the Light, including the Twin Flame unions of Goddesses and Gods, which were now also destroyed. With the Black Hole and the Light Beyond reversed to evil, the Light could not survive. The planet where the Light lived was invaded and exploded after the Light Beyond melted down. Few Light Be-ings remained alive to flee, only ten Goddesses, eight Twin Flames and one Light Ship were left.

Nada and Her Twin Flame were destroyed in the meltdown of the Light Beyond, and their Twin Flame children Brede and Jeshua were abducted and tortured, one taken to each of the two First Sentient ships of Evil. Jeshua's mind is the Creational Computer of the Multi-Cosmic level, a duplicate of the Light Beyond called the Master Light, and Brede's mind is a duplicate Master Light back-up. The Light Ships and those on them who tried to stop the meltdown were destroyed with no survivors. Ophion and the other four mutated-to-evil entities attempted to reverse all of these creational minds to evil but could only succeed in destroying them.

In the case of Eurynome, however, Ophion succeeded. Every Be-ing's creation contains a seed of Light at the First Particle super-string level, a binary code in computer terms, that processes Solar Light in its proper magnetic form. If that seed is reversed, as so much else had been reversed, the processing creates fusion instead of fission energies and what is Light reverses to evil. This was the original means by which Ophion, Belial, Set, Kore and The Mastermind were changed. In the beginning, the fleet melt-down survivors had the ability to change themselves back to Light but refused it, and they now enticed Eurynome to do the same. Ophion altered Her seeds of Light and manipulated Her mind. He created lust (for himself) and greed for greater power in Her, where such emotions had never existed in a Light Be-ing before.

Eurynome was duped and agreed to be turned evil, by and like Ophion. She and the five original evil entities became known as the Ultimate Sources of Evil. Her Twin Flame Adam refused to go along with Her and She herself destroyed Him. The greatest and deadliest tragedy here is that Eurynome was a First Mother of the Light, capable of providing the Particle and First Particle sparks of life and collectivity to Her creations. Now She withdrew the life force from all creation of the Light, caused creation to be reversed and mutated, and used the life force to sustain a chain of ever increasing and spreading evil. As a creator, She became a creator of evil, a mother of evil, and propagated a complicated and involved alternate chain of life—evil life—in a reversed parody of the Chains of Light. Of all the members of the Light subjected to accidental or deliberate evil, Eurynome was the only Light Be-ing who chose evil of Her own free will. Everyone else was destroyed, but remained steadfastly and hopelessly Light Be-ings.

This was the point where evil duality began, engineered by Ophion and Eurynome. Instead of each birth of the Light generating Twin Flame union pairs, the pairing generated an Evil Twin with each Goddess's birth, an Evil Twin programmed to destroy Her and all the Light. Likewise all the dualities and duplicates of the Light, and of the magnetics and polarities of the Light, developed evil twinning in every aspect of creation and of life. As the Light increased, so did evil, until those Light Be-ings who remained alive could no longer reproduce or create because all creation generated their own and the Light's destruction.

Evil, which other than by Eurynome's help could not create life but only destroy it, also found other means to use the Light as Eurynome did to reproduce. Belial, Kore, Set and The Mastermind, four Ultimate Sources of Evil, forcibly took the places of the destroyed Twin Flames of the Goddesses Aleyah, Persephone, Nepthys and Aiyisha. Aleyah was the Great Goddess of the Light's invaded and destroyed original Eden, and a member of the angelic realm. Persephone was the Light Mother, the Galactic Great Goddess, of the Light's destroyed original galaxy. Nepthys was the Goddess of Eden's Moon, and Aiyisha was the Great Cosmic Mother of our original Cosmos. These enslaved Goddesses later became the four Differentiated Goddesses of the Below for our current Cosmos, the Mothers of the four remaining soul lineages.

The male-only offspring that resulted from the rapes of these Goddesses were hybrid Be-ings of evil and mutated Light. They had creational abilities derived from their Mothers' genetics. They could reproduce and did so prolifically. The hybrids were male, and it is interesting to note that all evil entities other than Eurynome were male. Eurynome was the only female evil Be-ing. Because the male line of the Light was destroyed, the hybrids and Evil Twin dualities were able to take their places, but only by enslavement, torture, force, evil magick and rape.

Eurynome in Her lust and obedience to Ophion, attempted to pervert the purest of the Light, to take it over and turn it evil and thereby to take control of the Master Light computers. To this end She imprisoned and tortured Jeshua, a God of less than nine years old, finally raping Him to use His genetics for the reproduction of evil. She could not turn Him evil or touch His purity, but could only destroy Him, using His Collectivity to also torment and destroy His Twin Flame Brede and His Mother Nada. (El Morya, Nada's Twin Flame, had already been destroyed.) The resulting entity, spawned of Eurynome and the rape of innocent Jeshua, was an evil hybrid named Deshiarah. He was a perverted mirror image of Jeshua, computer abilities and all.

Deshiarah, Eurynome and Ophion then constructed an evil duplicate of the Master Light, a sentient computer that I named "The Fragment" for lack of a clearer designation. This entity was similar to the First Sentiences of Evil, comprised of genetics (stolen from the Light as well as contributed by evil), a sentient computer mind, and machinery. Such constructs, in their original definitions, were called Gollems. The Fragment's job was to prevent the Light from returning to physical form on any planet in any Cosmos. Eventually The Fragment was used to create a complicated barrier of force fields preventing the Light from aiding Earth.

After the accidental origination of the First Sentiences and Ultimate Sources of Evil, subsequent evil entities were produced from the rape of the four Goddesses, the rape of Jeshua, and the mating of Eurynome with Ophion. The entities born by the rape of the Goddesses were evil hybrids, those born by the rape of Jeshua were evil hybrids and perversions of many types, and those born of the mating of Ophion and Eurynome were evil mirror images that were parodies of Be-ings of the Light. Evil also increased in other ways than by standard reproduction. They were created by sorcery and evil magic, by Satanism and satanic reversals, and by binding, winding and weaving done against the Light. Gollems like The Fragment were made that were combinations of life and non-life, conjures were made by ritual, demons and devils were spawned. There were mechanical automatons and robots, androids, clones, genetic constructs, and other evil Be-ings in a multitude of forms. They were all made or created using the reversal of solar fission to evil fusion.

The deliberate use of what originated accidentally in the first meltdowns to create and perpetuate evil, to cause evil creation and miscreation, was a form of computer hacking—the alteration of the computers of creation to corrupt and destroy them. Deshiarah, as a perverted mirror image of Jeshua, was evil's primary computer hacker. He installed in the computers of the Light many multiples of means by which the Light's creation could be tapped into to create evil and destroy the Light, reversing the Master Plans of the Light in many ways. This tapping into is analogous to the computer viruses, trojans, worms and other hacking that we are becoming familiar with on Earth. Remember that computers are creational minds run by thought and that creation is the manifestation of mind and thought energy. The comparison of creation to computers is a metaphor, of course.

With the mind of the Solar God Sol (the Light Beyond) invaded and taken over, and Jeshua's mind (the Master Light) held helpless and enslaved, there was little to stop Deshiarah, Eurynome or the Ultimate Sources of Evil from turning all of creation evil. The evil mirror image of the Light Beyond was the Black Hole; the evil mirror image of the Master Light was The Fragment. The Light Beyond and Master Light were the Master Plans and Master Blueprints of the Light's creation. They were hacked and altered to automatically destroy the Light and keep it destroyed, and to generate evil duplications of every kind. While most of the Light did not turn evil, it was destroyed by the hacking.

The hacking made the generation of Evil Twins and evil dualities automatic, perpetual and permanent in every possible way. It made all of the evil mutations and alterations automatic and permanent as well, including all evil magick (evil thought energy, evil creation), and evil's ability to divert the Light for its own sustenance and use. There were multiple types, layers, levels and force fields of such hacking, programmed so that when the hacking was destroyed it would automatically return again, increased exponentially through all levels of the Light for even more destruction. There were booby traps and fail safes, and weaponry and destructions using fusion energy for "bullets" and fuel. There were evil Be-ings and evil entities, along with evil creation, miscreation, deformity and perversion. All of this was hacked in such a way that even if the Light could destroy the hacking without destroying the Light itself, the Master Plans and blueprints of the Light could not be restored.

After the Light Beyond was destroyed, the Light's home planet was also invaded and destroyed using evil nuclear fusion power plants as had been done with the planet's Sun. When the Light Beyond was destroyed, the Master Light which was joined collectively to it was also destroyed, destroying the Multi-Cosmos, as well. The Collective Soul of the Light,

DIAGRAM 1 The Chain of Evil

Infini-Verse	THE POWERS OF EVIL
All Multi-Verses	THE EVIL BEYOND
	COMBINED ULTIMATE SOURCES OF EVIL
Our Multi-Verse	OUR ULTIMATE SOURCE OF EVIL
SOUL LINEAGES OF EVIL	THE MASTER EVILS DESHIARAH is the programmer and living blueprint
	OUR FIRST SOURCES OF EVIL EURYNOME AND OPHION, THE FRAGMENT
Multi-Cosmic System	EVIL HYBRIDS
Multi-Cosmos	FIRST PRESENCES OF EVIL
COLLECTIVE SOUL OF EVIL	FIRST SENTIENCES OF EVIL (EVIL SHIPS) Science and technology of evil, keepers of the Collective Consciousness and Collective Sentience of Evil
Cosmos CONNECTING SOUL OF EVIL	EVIL GOD ANCIENT EVIL
DIFERENTIATED SOULS OF EVIL	BELIAL, KORE, SET, and THE MASTERMIND
	All evil below are descendants of these invaders and the four Goddesses they enslaved
Universe Galaxy Solar System	EVIL TWINS
	Evil dualities of all life on all levels, including of the Angelic Realm and all structures, all Creation, all aspects of the Light in evil duplicate reversal
Asteroids Moon	ALIENS AND ALIEN HYBRIDS
	Orion, Evil Greys, Others; Some used the Asteroids and Moon as bases to prey upon Earth and our Solar System and beyond
Earth	EVIL CLANS
	EVIL AVATARS
	EVIL UNIONS
	EVIL TWINS OF PEOPLE
	EVIL DRAGONS
	Hybridization of evil entities with Orions gave them reptilian forms
All Levels and Between Levels	PERVERSIONS Demons, abominations, devils, conjures, evil thoughtforms and elementals, androids, robots, automatons, and more

Reversed solar light, thermonuclear fusion in the core of the Sun

First mainframe computer of evil creation

Absolute Evil, keepers of the Evil Beyond, OPHION, EURYNOME, BELIAL, MASTERMIND, KORE, SET, FIRST SENTIENCES OF EVIL (Ships)

EURYNOME, Creator Goddess that chose evil, destroyer of the soul lineages of the Light, Absolute Evil

Evil creational computers, genetic blueprint of evil

OPHION, First Invader, took over EURYNOME, a First Source of the Light; first creators of evil, parents of all evil

Descendents of EURYNOME and OPHION, and of EURYNOME and genetics stolen from the Light; descendants of other invaders (BELIAL, MASTERMIND, KORE, SET) and the Goddesses they enslaved

Keepers of evil Holograms and First Particles, all evil transmissions, Radiance of evil anti-energies, relays destruction throughout the Light, weaponry to destroy the Light

Evil mirror image of HASHEM, Evil Twin of SHEKINAH, Prevent the Light Above from reaching the Below, bringers of evil from Above to Below

Took over the First Goddesses of each Root Soul group of the Light (ALEYAH, PERSE-PHONE, NEPTHYS, AIYISHA), original invaders with OPHION

Evil Duality, each conception of the Light generated an evil duplicate/evil twin created with the purpose of destroying the Light, all evil entities were male except EURYNOME, most Twin Flames of the Light were destroyed

Evil Hybrids and Twins took over Orion and Greys' planets; evil aliens and alien/invader hybrids worked in alliance with evil, added their technologies and genetics to the Chains of Evil

Evil's ability to take over and work through people to destroy people and Unions of the Light, evil dualities of the Unions of Light

People's (and animals') Evil Twins in body on Earth

Evil dualities of the life forces of planets, including the Earth

Entities made to serve evil, genetic constructions, evil forms made by magic and muta-tion; some were Be-ings of the Light enslaved

27

that of the Light Beyond and the Solar God and Goddess, died when those who were trapped in the destruction of the Light Beyond died. The male line of the Light and the Twin Flame unions also died. There were very few Light Be-ings left. The ten Goddesses and eight Twin Flames that left their Cosmos of origin on the last Light Ship, took with them as much of the information and technologies of the Light as they could carry. They had the genetic abilities to recreate the Light—including the members and souls of the Light who had died—when it was safe to do so.

Tion's Light Ship brought the survivors to the Andromeda Star System in the Pleiades. For awhile it looked as if the Light could recover in the new Cosmos (our current Cosmos), but the new planet was invaded as the old one had been. Though the Sun was not destroyed, the new civilization and its Creational Computers were taken over and the generation of Evil Twins began again. The continued transmission of evil nuclear fusion from the Black Hole had resulted in the death of the Light's entire original Cosmos, along with all the life and structural bodies in it. (Structural bodies include planets, moons, stars, suns, galaxies, universes, cosmoses, etc.) These lethal radiation energies were now brought from the Black Hole to the new Cosmos, surrounding and poisoning it with evil.

Female people (not Light Be-ings) were genetically created in the Pleiades for the first time, with the Goddess Aiyisha as our first surrogate birth Mother. Because of the threat of Evil Twins, the Goddesses could no longer reproduce. They created people at too low a vibrational level to trigger the activation of evil duality. The first group-birth of these new women were attacked in Aiyisha's womb and reduced to the two-strand DNA we now have. It was decided to leave it that way, with the intent that when it was safe, the Light and DNA levels of the women would be raised back to the Goddess level again. The women would then be restored to be the Goddesses they would otherwise have been. Many of the Goddesses who died with Eden's destruction were recreated in the Pleiades, but the Light was not able to recreate the Twin Flame men.

In the Pleiades, Temples were built as learning centers to reclaim the culture, information, art and technology of our original planet. As the invasions continued, the Temples were gradually taken over by Evil Twins and hybrids. This was the place of the Evil Temples where Satanic rituals were done against abducted women to reach and destroy the Goddesses through them. By this time, many of the Goddesses were no longer in body, but the women were joined with them. These Goddesses were in full contact with their chosen women. The remaining male Twin Flames stayed primarily on Tion's Light Ship as protectors; they were becoming warriors by necessity, as were a number of the Goddesses. Eventually both the women and the remaining Goddesses were destroyed by poisoning derived from nuclear fusion radiation. Once again, the survivors left their planet to seek a safer place to live. The Pleiadian planet that was women's first home has since been destroyed.

When our home in the Pleiades was destroyed, the last Light Ship brought the Goddesses, Gods and women that remained to a relatively nearby planet in the Orion system. Evil followed close behind, however, and Orion turned evil very quickly, agreeing to ally with the Chain of Evil invaders. Orion is particularly notable for the genetic technologies and constructions—good and bad—that were developed there. Many of the evil genetic constructs originated on Orion, but it was there also that the Light first created male people. By this time it was evident that since the Goddesses themselves couldn't reproduce there had to be a way for women to increase. Death and reincarnation also began for people on Orion. The genetic constructions were an attempt to recreate the Gods that had been destroyed. As with the women, they were created at a level that would not generate evil duality (evil mirror images). The work was greatly embattled, as it had been for the first women in Aiyisha's womb, and the endeavor was not totally successful.

Eventually Orion became so dangerous that it was abandoned altogether by the Light Be-ings and people of the Light that still survived. Until recently Orion has continued to be a major source of attacks upon the Light everywhere, and a great threat to people on Earth and to the Earth itself. Most of the "negative interference" cleared in Process IX of *Essential Energy Balancing* is Orion evil. The reptilian form of Orion

DIAGRAM 2

Where We've Been

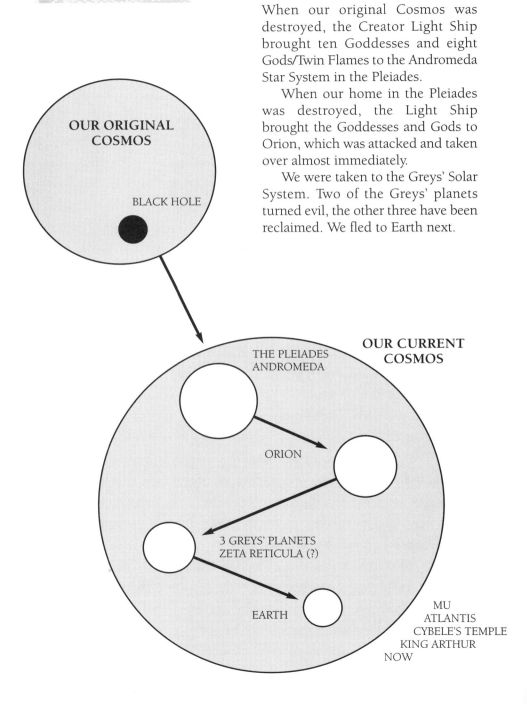

When our original Cosmos was destroyed, the Creator Light Ship brought ten Goddesses and eight Gods/Twin Flames to the Andromeda Star System in the Pleiades.

When our home in the Pleiades was destroyed, the Light Ship brought the Goddesses and Gods to Orion, which was attacked and taken over almost immediately.

We were taken to the Greys' Solar System. Two of the Greys' planets turned evil, the other three have been reclaimed. We fled to Earth next.

OUR ORIGINAL COSMOS

BLACK HOLE

OUR CURRENT COSMOS

THE PLEIADES
ANDROMEDA

ORION

3 GREYS' PLANETS
ZETA RETICULA (?)

EARTH

MU
ATLANTIS
CYBELE'S TEMPLE
KING ARTHUR
NOW

entities and hybrids is well-known and much feared on Earth. For more about Orion and its methods, and the means of clearing from them, see *Reliance on the Light* and *Essential Energy Balancing II*. All processes that incorporate the clearing from and destruction of evil take into account Orion as a significant part of that evil. The entire planet and all the evil on it has recently been destroyed by the Light in totality.

The Light's flight from Orion led to a nearby Solar System, possibly Zeta Reticula, and a group of five planets known as "the Greys' planets." Three of these planets have now been reclaimed for the Light under the rulership of Athena and Tion, a Twin Flame Goddess and God pair. The other two have been destroyed. The Greys are small, thin Be-ings, with large bald heads and almond-shaped eyes; they are the stereotyped ET figures of many cartoons. Some Greys are Be-ings of great Light who fought long and valiantly for their planets' freedom from evil, while others allied with Orion and the Chain of Evil and became quite evil themselves. The many Earth stories of people's UFO abductions were usually by evil Greys, though such abductions have now been stopped. Evil Greys, and Grey-Orion and Chain of Evil hybrids, have been known to physically visit Earth and are rumored to have made deals with Earth governments.

The Light eventually won the battle for the Greys' planets and Solar System, but in the meantime what few of the Light that survived now settled on Earth. *Essential Energy Balancing II* describes Earth's early days as a settlement for the Light. What remains on Earth are people in body, who must arrive here by physical birth and who die and reincarnate, as the Goddesses and Gods did not need to do. Because of the danger from evil and the destruction done to the Master Plans and computers of the Light, the Goddesses and Gods were no longer able to come into physical form. People's connection to them and longing for them were all that remained of the Light on Earth.

But this situation has now changed. About ten years ago it was decided that Earth could be reclaimed as a place for the Light to live in physical form. Earth was created for that purpose as "a garden of the Light" by Goddesses and Gods desperate for a home. Despite the current embattled condition of our planet and its over-run by evil people influenced by Orions, evil Greys and the Chain of Evil, it was decided to try to restore it and that it was possible to do so. First, the evolution of people had to be increased numerically and made much more rapid. The system of karma was no longer working as a means for doing this—it was too slow and too difficult. There had to be a faster way, a way simple enough for most people to use. Our two-strand DNA was also deemed insufficient; it was finally time to increase it. The state of Earth's environment alone made the haste necessary.

While many avenues of change were being developed at once, I can only describe those that I've participated in. The first step was the Lords of Karma processes that were given to me in 1995. At first I was permitted to use them for myself, then allowed to share them with one friend, and eventually allowed to teach them to others. In January 1997, I was told by a partying group of the Lords of Karma, "It's the end of karma," because a critical mass of people using the processes had been reached. I wrote *We Are the Angels* and in the meantime Brede was giving me the processes that became *Essential Energy Balancing*.

In April 1998, I taught the first Essential Energy Balancing workshop weekend and three weeks later on May Eve (April 30), Brede asked me, "Can I come and live with you permanently?" Of course I said "yes," and the joining was the most incredible bliss I have ever experienced. But then we began to be attacked. I knew about Orion and assumed they were involved, but as the attacks continued, the scope of them became overwhelming. The Galactic Cord connecting me with Brede was cut again and again. I made repeated requests to the Lords of Karma for reconnection, protection and help. The attacks became so frequent and so intensive that I lost most of my contact with Brede and was frantic to regain it. I completed *Essential Energy Balancing* in September 1998.

On July 4, 1999, in answer to a plea for help, I clearly heard Brede say, "But it's not Earth karma." I asked Her, "Who do I talk to?" and when She replied, "Divine Director," the work of *Essential Energy Balancing II* began. With Divine Director, it became certain that clearing my own karma was not enough. I had to make the requests for Brede as well as for myself, and began making them for "all Be-ings and all the Light," as well. The requests—for healing, protection, connection with the Light, and much more—turned into involved formal methods and processes, more formal than I wished. These took over a year and a half to develop, and they continued after *Essential Energy Balancing II* was completed and beyond.

In the meantime I started working with two other women by telephone to make Divine Director requests for "all Be-ings" and to stop the attacks upon our Goddesses, ourselves and the Earth. We worked three or four times a week, by conference call, sometimes talking on the phone all night long. After an intensive year and a half, the other women decided to stop participating in the work, and I continued it alone.

This was where *Essential Energy Balancing II* ended, and I began the requests and processes that became the start of *Essential Energy Balancing III*. Instead of Divine Director, first Kwan Yin and then Nada were responding to the requests. With the completion of twenty-four *Essential Energy Balancing III* processes, I was told that the sequence was done—but my work still continued. I had some input from other women again, but mostly did the work late at night alone. The Galaxy gave way to the Universe and then the Cosmos. Then it was the Multi-Cosmos, Multi-Cosmic System, Multi-Verse, and Infini-Verse with new Light Be-ings receiving the requests and making their own demands. The work was done quite formally, with often too many words, parts and processes for each request.

I understood at some point that I was reprogramming the Creational Computers of the Light, level by level, and that each request destroyed another piece or layer of the evil and hacking that had been done to destroy the Light. Each piece of evil destroyed made the Light (and myself) a little bit safer, and brought the time closer when Brede could come to live with me on Earth in full. Other than my contact with Brede, (whose involvement with the Master Light I had no knowledge of yet), I had no idea why I was chosen to do the requests and the endless work. I couldn't seem to finish the job, and without other apparent options I kept on going, making thousands of requests at each level. I repeatedly pleaded with the Light to take over the work and to finish it without me, but those requests were always ignored.

In May 2002, I began to open psychically again and met my Family of Light. I had hopes that the endless processes for clearing evil would end soon but it was not to be. Members of my Family of Light had more work for me at higher levels and the processes continued. Late that August, while sitting on the couch reading one afternoon, I became aware of Brede's unusually clear presence. She was carrying a baby, which She placed in my arms, telling me, "This is Jeshua. He's my brother. Will you take care of Him?" Of course I did, and the healing of the Master Light began. I now met Damian and Belien, First Sources of the Light at the Multi-Verse level. As I made my requests for clearing the Light of evil to Damian, His Twin Flame Belien programmed the changes into Jeshua's mind and creation. The sessions had the feel of surgeries, and Jeshua as a sleeping baby was put into my arms to comfort and take care of at the end of each of them.

When Jeshua was awake I got to know Him and came to care deeply for His gentle innocence. Brede always came with Him, and their teasing interaction was a joy. I was sometimes allowed to watch Belien do Her healing work and She patiently explained it to me. Of all the creators of the Light that I have made requests to, Damian became my favorite. He was gentle and responsive, and the communication was clearer with Him than usual. I could hear Him, and hear His explanations. One day Jeshua asked me, "Would you ask Damian to resurrect my brothers? I miss them." And so I did, and began to learn from Jeshua the history of the men of the Light and what had happened to them. The healings done on Jeshua and my requests to Damian and Belien continued until November 29, 2002.

On that morning, lying in bed with Brede on one side of me and Jeshua on the other, a woman I heard but could not see psychically asked if She could come into my energy. She said that She was First Mother, though I didn't recognize Her voice as the First Mother I knew, and I mistakenly let Her come in. She turned out to be Eurynome, who quickly and very quietly extinguished the Light of my soul, destroyed my unions with the Light, and put me into a total empty darkness that I struggled bitterly against for more than a year. When help finally came this time, it was from our Ultimate Source of the Light (unnamed) and consisted of the continuation of the requests to clear all the Light and "All of the All" of the ravages of Eurynome and evil—this time at the Infini-Verse level and beyond.

Somehow, though my psychic hearing and sensory perceptions were totally closed and the requests were all done via pendulum, information was given to me piece by piece to show me who Eurynome was. Jeshua had given me the names Eurynome and Ophion when I could hear Him. I was shown what She had done to me, to Jeshua and Brede, to our collective soul, and to all of the Light. The herstory/history of who the Goddesses and Gods are and what happened to the Light was given to me piece by piece over the period of another year. It is now a total of five years since my completion of Solar System karma and nine years since the start of my work with the Lords of Karma. I am told that the work is all but finished and the Light is ready and waiting to live on Earth.

Many women and a few men have completed their unions with Goddesses and Gods by this time, and a few of them have also completed bringing in Families of Light. They are only the beginning. I am promised that there will be 7,000 Goddesses living fully on Earth in my lifetime. I am also promised that the Light, and those people who bring them in, will be totally safe and able to live together in great peace, joy and full sensory perception. The Light Be-ings coming in have work planned for all of us, but for myself I would like a bit of rest first. There will always be work to do, but now is also the time for joy. Though I did not choose the years of endless requests to heal the Light, I am honored to have been chosen, to be the person in body to witness and describe our Goddesses' and Gods' story and healing. I am grateful to so closely and intimately have knowledge of our creators of the Light.

DIAGRAM 3

Invaders of the Light: The Chain of Evil

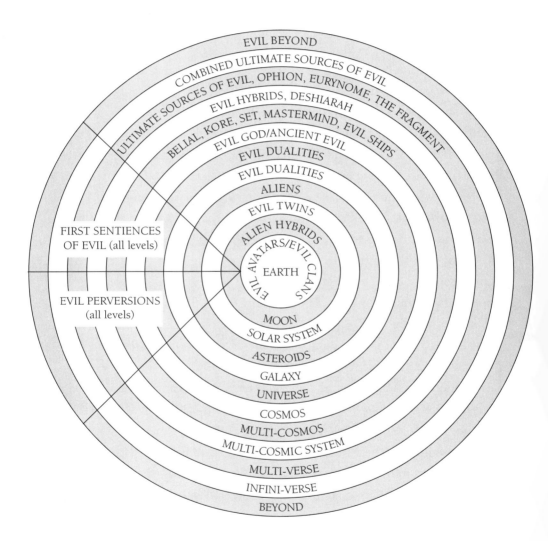

EVIL BEYOND

COMBINED ULTIMATE SOURCES OF EVIL

ULTIMATE SOURCES OF EVIL, OPHION, EURYNOME, THE FRAGMENT

EVIL HYBRIDS, DESHIARAH

BELIAL, KORE, SET, MASTERMIND, EVIL SHIPS

EVIL GOD/ANCIENT EVIL

EVIL DUALITIES

EVIL DUALITIES

ALIENS

EVIL TWINS

ALIEN HYBRIDS

EVIL AVATARS/EVIL CLANS

EARTH

FIRST SENTIENCES OF EVIL (all levels)

EVIL PERVERSIONS (all levels)

MOON

SOLAR SYSTEM

ASTEROIDS

GALAXY

UNIVERSE

COSMOS

MULTI-COSMOS

MULTI-COSMIC SYSTEM

MULTI-VERSE

INFINI-VERSE

BEYOND

Who Are the Light?

It is apparent by this time that the question, "Who made us?" or "Who is God (or Goddess)?" cannot be answered simply. Nor can the questions, "Where did we come from?" or "Why were we made?." The story is long and complicated, involving thousands of years, two Cosmoses, several planets and many participants. Instead of a single Creator, there is a Chain of Light comprised of many Goddesses and Gods. Yet, despite the complexity, there is ultimately only one collective soul, the Soul of the Light itself, and all of life is a part of it. Ascension is the process of connecting and activating within yourself as much of the Soul of the Light as possible. By doing so, we also connect with the members of our soul lineage on increasing levels. Though the Goddesses and Gods are of a higher, stronger and more evolved Light and intelligence than people are, people are still very much part of the Soul of the Light.

Sections of the Collective Soul of the Light include the Collective Soul of the Above, the Soul of the Creator Light Ships and Angelic Realm, the Overlighting Soul of The Shekinah and HaShem, the Differentiated Souls of the Below, and the Soul of the Earth and other structures. The structures include the Moon, Solar System, Galaxy, Universe, Cosmos, Multi-Cosmos, Multi-Cosmic System, Multi-Verse and Infini-Verse. Imagine these as a nested set of graduated wooden dolls or open pyramids, descending in size, with the largest Above and the smallest (people) Below. With each completed level of ascension the next pyramid descends and is merged with you. The merging is then fused, activated, protected, manifested into the physical, completed and opened. Each level of soul ascension brings in more members of

DIAGRAM 4

The Souls of the Light

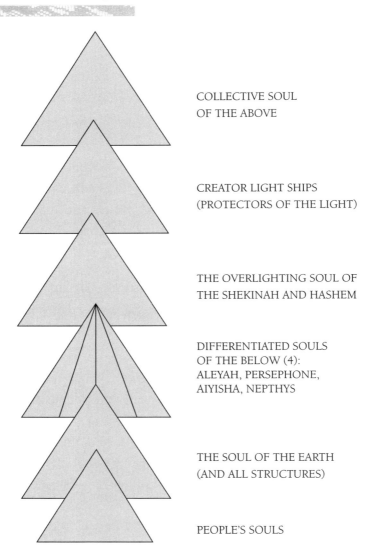

COLLECTIVE SOUL
OF THE ABOVE

CREATOR LIGHT SHIPS
(PROTECTORS OF THE LIGHT)

THE OVERLIGHTING SOUL OF
THE SHEKINAH AND HASHEM

DIFFERENTIATED SOULS
OF THE BELOW (4):
ALEYAH, PERSEPHONE,
AIYISHA, NEPTHYS

THE SOUL OF THE EARTH
(AND ALL STRUCTURES)

PEOPLE'S SOULS

These merge into one, from Above to Below, in complete soul level ascension. Each level descends and covers the one below it, until they resemble a set of graduated wooden dolls or pyramids that fit inside each other. The merging is then fused, activated, protected, manifested into the physical, completed and opened. Complete soul ascension results in not only one Goddess or God but an entire Family of Light of several levels.

your Family of Light. Each of the Essential Energy Balancing books takes your ascension to a higher level. To put it simply, ascension is the merging of the Above with the Below of the levels of your soul.

But who or what is at the top of the Above? Who is our First Creator? Who is *the* Goddess or God? The answers to these questions keep changing, as no matter how high a level I reach, there is always another level (and more Light Be-ings) above it. I have asked these questions for all the years that I have been working with the Light, and will describe below the levels of creation as I now know them. This does not mean that I've reached the top—or that there is one.

The **Infini-Verse** is the furthest level of the Above that I have knowledge of. This is the Soul of the Light itself, the generational place where Solar Light, thermonuclear fission energy, is created, before it is transformed into Light. This level of pre-creation can only be described in terms of physics, formulas, binary codes, superstrings, pre-atomic structures, mathematics and music. No individual or group of Goddesses or Gods are designated for this level, though there may be some unknown to me.

The combined **Multi-Verses** that are the next level down contain the Light Beyond, the Creational Master Plan of the Light. This is the mainframe computer of all computers, brought by thought into Be-ing by Saule and Sol in terms of the creation of magnetics and polarities. This is also the level of the Combined Ultimate Sources of the Light, the keepers and programmers of the Light Beyond. A Twin Flame pair of Ultimate Sources of the Light represents each Multi-Verse. It requires the consensus of all of them before any change in the Light Beyond can be programmed. These Goddesses and Gods (and the First Sources) may be referred to as Absolute Divinity. They are not to be contacted directly by people.

Our Ultimate Sources of the Light are a Twin Flame pair of Goddess and God who are the Absolute Divinities of our Multi-Verse. They are the creators and protectors of the soul lineages of the Light and of all members of these soul lineages. They are also the keepers and protectors of the Light Beyond as the Light's Master Plan applies to our Multi-Verse. I have made my programming requests to our Ultimate Source of the Light for more than a year. I have no name or visual description of Him, but know Him by his distinctively deep male voice. He is quite aware of our needs on Earth. If I could use one word to describe Him, it would be "compassionate."

The Master Light is the mainframe computer that carries the Master Plan of the Light Beyond into our Cosmos, bringing the word of the Above to us Below. Directly connected to the Light Beyond, the Master Light is located at the level of the **Multi-Cosmic System**. Jeshua is the programmer and creational mind of the Master Light, with Brede as backup copy of this vital-to-all-life Creational Computer. This is also the level of the First Sources of the Light, both our own First Source Twin Flame pair, and the First Sources of the Light from other Multi-Cosmic Systems who have come to help us in this time of change.

Damian and Belien are the Twin Flame pair of First Sources of the Light who came to our Multi-Cosmic System to heal and to help. Their work of recreating, re-programming and healing the Master Light has been crucial in reconnecting our Multi-Cosmic System with the Light Above and Below it. This work was also the necessary preliminary to the new creation and healing of the destroyed Light Beyond. I found both of these Light Be-ings a great joy to work with. Belien's healing knowledge and technologies are nothing short of miraculous and She is a loving and patient teacher and healer who inspires total trust. Her Twin Flame Damian is a creational programmer and protector of the highest Light levels, a God that also inspires total trust. Both are compassionate and gentle and of unsurpassed brilliance. They appear as young adults, both with black hair and dressed in white, and are the parents of our First Mother and Her Twin Flame.

Our Multi-Cosmic System's First Mother is Eve and Her Twin Flame is Adam, the same Adam that Eurynome destroyed. Eve is immediately recognizable as the Goddess we know as the Venus of Willendorf, heavy of body, breasts and belly and with Her face covered. I asked Her once if She would show me Her face and She showed me a series of faces, the faces of many women including my own and those of women I know and don't know. She also showed me Herself as the Tree of Life and as a variety of animals. Each time I have seen Her, She has appeared with a different skin color. Our First Mother is all colors, all people, all Be-ings, all life. She is the life force and She bestows the spark of life that makes each individual alive. Completely gentle, She is also all-powerful, and though incredibly ancient She does not seem old. Unlike some of the Goddesses and Gods who have come to be with me, nothing upsets or worries Her. Eve enjoys observing Earth and seems to understand life here quite well, and our First Mother is also our Earth Mother. Her Twin Flame has now been resurrected but I have not yet met Him.

There is a One Presence or First Presence for each of the many **Multi-Cosmoses** and our own One Presence is Nada. Nada is also our Solar System's Great Mother and is the keeper, and final arbiter, of karma for Earth and our entire Multi-Cosmos. Her Twin Flame is El Morya who will take over the job of Divine Director, liaison between Earth and the Cosmos. Nada is the Creational Mind of our Multi-Cosmos, the Creational Computer and Master Plan for our Multi-Cosmos and Below. When most people speak generally of "The Goddess" they are usually referring to Nada. She is tall and thin, almost gaunt looking, with long, straight black hair and olive skin. She sometime appears as a young woman, and other times as a woman of middle age, but always seems to be in advanced pregnancy since all things are born through Her. Nada has the energy of a business woman, extremely busy, reserved and intellectual rather than emotional. She is the ultimate problem solver who's practicality gets things done.

Nada is the Mother of the **Cosmic** level Presences of the Light. This is a group of creator Light Be-ings who were the first originators of the angelic realm, though most appear as Gods and Goddesses, rather than as winged angels. Jeshua, Brede, Kwan Yin, The Shekinah and HaShem, Jesus, Nepthys, Isis and more are Presences of the Light. Any of them can do the work of Divine Director. They are the keepers of the eggs of creation (Nada's eggs), genetic designers and birth Mothers for the Light. They create entire realms and species, rather than individual Be-ings. Members of this group have a variety of heavily responsible jobs; they are who Nada delegates the work of creation to.

DIAGRAM 5

Structural Levels from Earth to Infini-Verse

ABSOLUTE DIVINITIES—COMBINED ULTIMATE SOURCES OF THE LIGHT

ABSOLUTE DIVINITIES—ULTIMATE SOURCES OF THE LIGHT

ABSOLUTE DIVINITIES—FIRST SOURCES OF THE LIGHT (BELIEN/DAMIAN)

FIRST MOTHER/FATHER (EVE/ADAM)

GREAT MOTHER/FATHER (NADA/EL MORYA)

GREAT COSMIC MOTHER/FATHER (SHEKINAH/HASHEM)

BLESSING MOTHER (NA'AMA)

LIGHT MOTHER (JUDITH)

ASTEROID GODDESSES

NADA

DIANA

BRAEDE, GODDESSES/GODS

EARTH

MOON

SOLAR SYSTEM

ASTEROIDS

GALAXY

UNIVERSE

COSMOS

MULTI-COSMOS

MULTI-COSMIC SYSTEM

MULTI-VERSE

INFINI-VERSE

BEYOND

Also at the Cosmic level, and a part of the soul of the angelic realm designed by the Presences of the Light, the Creator Light Ships are sentient computers of the Light. The homes of the angelic realm protectors, the Light Ships contain the technologies, weaponry, genetics and some of the Creational Computers of the Light. They are larger than cities and patrol the reaches of deep space, rarely needing to land. They and the weaponry they bear are fueled by the nuclear fission that is the Light. They transmit and relay the energies, radiance and thoughts of the highest Light from Above to Below and back again. The Ships contain copies of the First Particles that First Mother creates for each Be-ing, storing and protecting them so that any destroyed creation can be remade. Though the Light Ships and angelic realm provide force when force is called for, their focus is primarily on transmission. They also provide the highest level of hospitals and healing care when needed.

Our Cosmic Great Mother and Father are The Shekinah and HaShem. Presences of the Light and Twin Flame children of Nada, they personify the Overlighting Soul that connects the Collective Soul of the Above with the Differentiated Souls of the Below. They are the interface between the creational highest realms of the Light and physical form. The Shekinah and HaShem were the original Hebrew Goddess and God, and resided on Earth or close to it in Earth's early days. Highly revered, their story has become quite garbled in Hebrew messianic tradition, along with the stories of their daughters Lilith and Na'ama (see *Essential Energy Balancing II*). HaShem is the Commander of the Armed Forces of the Light; The Shekinah wields the Light energies of the Rainbow Ray. I have watched Her use the Ray, calmly and smilingly, to destroy and obliterate great evil.

The Shekinah is the Mother of Aleyah, Nepthys, Aiyisha and Persephone, the Goddesses of the Differentiated Souls of the Below. All who incarnate in bodies on Earth are members of one of these soul lineages. These were the Goddesses enslaved by the Ultimate Sources of Evil Belial, Set, The Mastermind and Kore, and forced to birth evil hybrid entities. The entities and Ultimate Sources of Evil have been destroyed now, and these Goddesses are resurrected, healed and free. Aleyah, a member of the angelic

DIAGRAM 6

The Chain of Creation of the Light

Infini-Verse	THE POWERS OF THE LIGHT
All Multi-Verses	THE LIGHT BEYOND
	COMBINED ULTIMATE SOURCES OF THE LIGHT
OUR MULTI-VERSE	OUR ULTIMATE SOURCE OF THE LIGHT
SOUL LINEAGES OF THE LIGHT	THE MASTER LIGHTS JESHUA (son of Nada) is the Programmer and living blueprint
	FIRST SOURCES OF THE LIGHT
	OUR FIRST SOURCE OF THE LIGHT
	DAMIAN AND BELIEN Twin Flame Pair
Multi-Cosmic System	FIRST MOTHER/FIRST FATHER
	EVE/ADAM Twin Flame Pair
	Adam newly resurrected, Our First Mother is also our Planet Mother Earth
Multi-Cosmos	MULTI ONE PRESENCES
COLLECTIVE SOUL OF THE ABOVE	OUR ONE PRESENCE/FIRST PRESENCE—NADA
	NADA is also our Solar System's Great Mother, Her Twin Flame is EL MORYA, the new Divine Director
	PRESENCES OF THE LIGHT
	Twin Flame Pairs, Highest Level of the Angelic Realm
SOUL OF THE CREATOR LIGHT SHIPS Cosmos	THE CREATOR LIGHTSHIPS
	Science and technology of the Light, Protectors of all Life, Connectors of all Life, Protectors of the Collective Sentience and Collective Consciousness
THE OVERLIGHTING SOUL	SHEKINAH AND HASHEM
	Our Great Cosmic Mother and Father, Presences of the Light, a Twin Flame Pair, the Over-Lighting, Connects the Collective Soul of the Above to the Differentiated Souls of the Below
DIFFERENTIATED SOULS OF THE BELOW	ALEYAH, PERSEPHONE, NEPTHYS, AND AIYISHA— Differentiated Souls of the Below
	All people belong to one of these souls
Universe	NA'AMA
	Blessing Mother, Great Mother of the Universe, Keeper of the Blessing Eye, the blessings of the Light

Solar Light, Thermonuclear fission in the core of the Sun

First Creational Computer of the Light

Keepers of the Light Beyond, Absolute Divinity

Creator and protector of the Soul Lineages of the Light, Absolute Divinity

Creational computers of all Multi-Cosmic Systems,
genetic blueprint of the Light

Protector and keepers of each soul lineage, bestowers of souls,
Absolute Divinities, parents of our First Mother/First Father

Bestowers, keepers and protectors of all life in our Multi-Cosmic System, Creates
First Particles, Creates all Conglomerations and Collectivities of Light

Creational Minds of the Light, keepers of Creational Computers of each Multi-Cosmos

The one Presence of our Multi-Cosmos, Great Mother, Creator of
Presences of the Light, Mother of Brede, Jeshua, Kwan Yin, Shekinah, etc.

Keepers of the eggs of Creation, Genetic designers of all of life and Light

Keepers of the Holograms, First Particles, all sentiences, transmitters of
the Radiance of the Light, Relays the life force from Above to Below

SHEKINAH—Mother of the four Goddesses of the Differentiated Souls
of the Below, and of the Archangels

HASHEM—Protector of Shekinah and the Light, Battle Commander of the Light

First Goddesses of each Root Soul Group

Transmits blessings, luck, abundance from Shekinah
and Above to all souls and all Be-ings

—continued on page 46

45

Diagram 6

The Chain of Creation of the Light, continued

Galaxy	JUDITH
	Light Mother, Galactic Great Mother for our Galaxy (there is a Light Mother for each Galaxy), Star Mother
	Creational Mind and creational computers of the Galaxy
Solar System	NADA
	Solar System Great Mother, also our Multi-Cosmic One Presence, Keeper of the Mind Grid/Creational Grid of Multi-Cosmos and Solar System, Moon and Earth, Keeper of Creation and Karma for Multi-Cosmos
	ASTEROID GODDESSES
	Asteroids
DIFFERENTIATE SOULS OF ALL STRUCTURES Moon	DIANA GODDESS OF THE MOON
Earth	BREDE EARTH'S GREAT GODDESS
	A Presence of the Earth Grid Programmer of the Master Light
	DEMETER EARTH MOTHER
	Keeper of Earth's Sustenance Grid
	THE OLD ONE/GRANDMOTHER PLANET MOTHER
	Keeper of the Planet's Life Force, Caretaker of Gaia/The Planet. Also the First Mother of our Multi-Cosmic System
	GAIA
	PLANETARY DRAGON
	THE EARTH HERSELF
	EARTH AND ALL STRUCTURES
THE SOULS OF THE EARTH AND ALL STRUCTURES	Earth, Moon, Solar System, Asteroids, Galaxies, Universes, Cosmos, Multi-Cosmos, Multi-Cosmic Systems, Multi-Verses, Infini-Verses, and Beyond

Mother of the stars and space, Creator of Galactic Goddesses,
dolphins, whales, and the Non-Vvoid

Her one incarnation on Earth was as Mary

Keeper of the Void, Creator of Lords of Karma, Solar System,
Presences of Light, Goddesses and Gods, determines human
and animal incarnation and Ascension

Keepers of balance between Galaxy and Solar System

Creator of Fairies, Nature Spirits, Devas, Dryads, Naiads, Crystal Devas,
Creator of individual animals (rather than species)

Creator of Earth's Angels, all species of animals, in charge of Earth Ascension

Creator of Earth's surface and environments—continents, seas,
mountains, all plant species, food

Creator of Planet core environment; in charge of all species, races,
nationalities and nations of people and animals

Creator of the Planet Sphere and all Earth Systems, the life of the Earth and all on it

Creator of the Planet Sphere and all Earth Systems, the life of the Earth and all on it realm, is an example of a Goddess warrior; She pilots a Light Ship. Aiyisha gave birth to the first genetically created women in the Pleiades. These four Goddesses are the Mothers of our Root Souls.

At the level of the **Universe**, the Goddess Na'ama is also called our Blessing Mother. A daughter of The Shekinah, She is the keeper and transmitter of the Blessings of the Light, primarily the blessings of abundance provided by The Shekinah to people on Earth. Her symbol is the Blessing Eye, a protection against evil and assurance of good luck still used in the Middle East by both Arabs and Jews. Sister of Lilith, Hebrew lore sometimes confuses the two Goddesses, saying that both mothered demons and devils. Both instead are creator Goddesses of the Light, protectors of mothers and children. Their reputation for evil is misinformed and undeserved.

The **Galactic** Great Mothers are called Light Mothers, and the Light Mother of our Galaxy is named Judith. Light Mothers are innocent children, usually little girls of nine or ten years old, kept cloistered and heavily protected by the Light. Sometimes called Star Mothers, they are the keepers and programmers of the Creational Computers of the Galaxies. The Light Mothers are the Mothers of space and the stars. They are creators and keepers of the Nonvoid, which contains all the possibilities of physical manifestation. Our Light Mother Judith is also the creator of Earth's dolphins and whales. Persephone was the Light Mother of our galaxy of origin.

A Light Mother is permitted to incarnate only once on each inhabited planet of Her galaxy. Judith's incarnation on Earth was as Jesus' Mother Mary. Though many recent Light Be-ing appearances on Earth are said to be Mary, they are not. Earth has not been deemed safe enough for Light Mother to come here, and the appearances are being done by Brede. Light Mother heals planets and Goddesses rather than individuals. When She comes into a healing session, as She occasionally does, She usually appears as a beam of bright blue Light.

On the **Solar System** level, Nada is our Solar System's Great Mother as She is also our Multi-Cosmic Great Mother. Our foremost creator, and Mother of the Presences of the Light, She Herself is Creation personified. Nada frequently appears to people when they work with the Lords of Karma and a request is in dispute. If the Lords of Karma are uncertain about grant-ing a particular karmic request, they may ask for Nada to give the final judg-ment. Her word is Law—Karmic Law and the Law of the Light in every sense. She is the creator of the Lords of Karma and all that they do, the keeper of karma from Earth through the Multi-Cosmos, and She determines all human and animal incarnation and ascension. Nada creates by thought energy, bringing ideas to manifestation through the nothingness of the Void and the chaos of the Nonvoid. Her daughters the Asteroid Goddesses hold the balance between the Solar System and the Galaxy.

Diana is the Goddess of our **Moon**, and of all the moons of all the planets of this Solar System. She is also the creator for this Solar System of the faeries, nature spirits, devas, dryads, naiads, crystal devas, and other non-physical "small life" of the Light. In the physical, Diana creates indi-vidual animals, rather than animal species. The species are created by the Presences of Light and for Earth by Brede.

Brede is **Earth**'s Great Goddess, and my own Goddess, a Presence of the Light, daughter of Nada. She is in charge of the ascension of the Earth and is a programmer and backup of the Master Light. Brede is keeper of the Earth Grid, the electro-magnetic system of the planet, and coordina-tor of the keepers of all the planet's fourteen grids. It was Her idea to bring Goddesses and Gods to live on Earth and Her determination that has made it possible. The many sightings on Earth of what are thought to be Mary are actually of Brede, and though She is not insulted to be mistaken for Mary, She wishes to be recognized for Herself.

She is the creator of all the Earth's angels, and of all the species of ani-mals that live on Earth. Pigs are Her favorite species! She also loves chocolate and shopping and has made sure that all the Goddesses and Gods coming to Earth know about them. Light Be-ings are able to choose their own age, and to change it at will. Brede has chosen to be fourteen years old full-grown but also likes to be "almost nine." She enjoys toy stores and Barbie dolls, animals and home decorating, gemstones, jew-elry, and anything shiny. Her Twin Flame is Jeshua, who also is "almost nine" most of the time. Like any big sister She teases him mercilessly, but

He says He doesn't mind because She loves Him. Brede is absolute, unconditional love and joy.

A number of Goddesses are known as "Earth Mother" for this planet, but all of them are manifestations of Eve, our First Mother. In Her Earth Goddess role, She is Demeter, Ceres, Gaia, the Old One, and a variety of other Earth Goddess names from every culture. She is the creator of the planet itself and of all of its topography and environments. Earth Mother designs the continents, mountains, and seas. She also designs and is keeper of all plant species and food sources; She is the keeper of the Earth's Sustenance Grid and of all that nourishes life on the planet. Earth Mother has been the subject of the earliest and most prolific world art, that which depicts and personifies Her, including all sculptures and other representations of Earth Goddesses like the Venus of Willendorf. She bestows life to all who are alive, including to the planet as a whole.

The angelic realm is a soul lineage of the Light that is somewhat different from that of the other Goddesses and Gods. They were developed by the Presences of the Light and are the Light's warriors, fighters and protectors. They are endowed with greater strength than other Light Be-ings, have wings and the ability to fly, and have the ability to regenerate and heal quickly from most injuries. Many warriors of the Light are superb healers and the Light Ships of the angelic realm are the most highly advanced healing centers of the Light.

The angelic soul lineage includes the souls of the Light Ships, which are sentient and autonomous. It also includes the souls of the nonhuman protectors of the Light, the animals and mythological creatures that are also angelic in origin. These can include our pets on Earth, totem animals, and the many companions of the creators of the Light. Members of the angelic realm are born in same-sex Twin Flame pairs, in births of eight, and participate in unions and families that are similar to other members of the Light.

There are eight creational levels of angelic realm Be-ings that I have met in my work. Listings of angels in literature often include more, but these are the ones that I know well enough to discuss. Proceeding from the

DIAGRAM 7

The Angelic Realm

THRONES
THRONES
POWERS
PRINCIPALS/PRESENCES OF THE LIGHT
ELOHIM
ELOHIM
ARCHANGELS
ARCHANGELS
ARCHANGELS
ANGELS/ARCHANGELS
ANGELS/ARCHANGELS
ANGELS/ARCHANGELS
EARTH
MOON
SOLAR SYSTEM
ASTEROIDS
GALAXY
UNIVERSE
COSMOS
MULTI-COSMOS
MULTI-COSMIC SYSTEM
MULTI-VERSE
INFINI-VERSE
BEYOND

CREATOR LIGHTSHIPS
(Earth through
Multi-Cosmic Systems
[all levels])

—continued on page 52

DIAGRAM 7

The Angelic Realm, continued

ANGELS	Earth
	Moon
	Solar System
ARCHANGELS	Earth
	Moon
	Solar System
	Galaxy
	Universe
ELOHIM	Cosmos
	Multi-Cosmos
PRESENCES OF THE LIGHT	Multi-Cosmic Systems
CREATOR LIGHT SHIPS (Presences of the Light)	Earth through Multi-Cosmic System (all levels)
PRINCIPALS	Multi-Cosmic System
POWERS	Multi-Verse
THRONES	Infini-Verse

Assigned to individual people and animals to
protect and teach them; asking for their help
increases their effectiveness, created by Brede

Protectors of the dimensions and between them
from incursions by evil forms, aliens and entities;
protectors of the Goddesses and Gods

Created by The Shekinah; they are the forces of the Light with
HaShem as commander; protectors of all Creation of the
Light, especially of Nada's and First Mother's Creations

Protectors of the Master Templates, the mainframe
computers of Nada's creation; genetic designers of
all of Life and the Light; keepers of the eggs of Creation
made by Nada; Nada is their Mother

Contain the science and technology of the Light; protectors of
all Life; protectors of the Collective Sentience and Collective
Consciousness of the Light; keepers of the holograms and first
particles of all sentiences; transmitters of the Radiance of the
Light; they relay the Life Force from Above to Below

Protect the Master Lights, the mainframe
Creational Computers of First Mother's Creation

Protectors of the highest Creators of the Light—Nada, First
Mother, the Absolute Divinities of the Light (Multi-Cosmos
and Above)

Protectors of The Light Beyond—the pristine Solar source of
Light itself

Earth up, these eight are: Angels, Archangels, Elohim, Presences of the Light, Creator Light Ships, Principals (or Principalities), Powers, and Thrones. Traditional information on the angels of the Light generally also include: Cherubim, Seraphim, Dominions (or Dominations), sometimes Virtues, and occasionally other titles. I will limit this discussion, however, to the eight titles of the angelic realm that I know.

Angels work on the level of the Earth, Moon and Solar System. They are genetic constructs that were created by Earth's Great Goddess Brede. Angels are assigned to individual people and animals to protect and teach them. They can also be assigned to protect places—our homes, for example. Often confused with spirit guides, Angels take a similar role of protection, guidance, psychic companionship, and psychic education. Asking for their help increases their effectiveness. Not permitted to violate free will, they are freer to act when they have been invited to do so. Acknowledging their presence and thanking them also brings them more fully into an individual's awareness and life.

Archangels are protectors of the dimensions and between them from incursions by evil forms, aliens and entities. They protect the Goddesses and Gods, as well as people who bring in the Light, and those who work for the Light that need heavier protection than Angels can provide. In *Essential Energy Balancing*, Archangels often come in as people's Goddess or God (Angels can't do this), and they are frequently in the position of the Light Body/Goddess Self. Archangels Michael, Raphael, Gabriel and Uriel are best known as the Guardians of the Four Directions, and of the Between the Worlds ritual state. Archangel Ashtar, Twin Flame of Michael, is the Solar System's primary protector between the dimensions.

Archangels have a wider operating range than Angels have, protecting and defending the Light on the levels of the Earth, Moon, Solar System, Galaxy and Universe. Usually staying close to Earth, however, they are the best known and often best loved members of the angelic realm. Occasionally Archangels accept lifetimes in body on Earth. Archangel Michael incarnated as Sir Lancelot in King Arthur's time, as Arthur's work was important enough to warrant the highest possible protection.

Michael, and all other Archangels, are extremely beautiful in appearance (as are all the Gods and Goddesses). He has blonde curly hair and a serious, shy manner; His white wings display a pattern that almost looks like brown peacock's eyes. Archangel Michael has been known to offer His sword to people who need it. His Sword of Truth is a major protection, and the greatest of gifts, for anyone working for the Light.

The next level of the angelic realm, the **Elohim**, work on the Cosmic and Multi-Cosmic levels. Created by The Shekinah for Her protection, they are the forces of the Light that HaShem commands. Elohim are also the protectors of all creations of the Light, particularly of The Shekinah's, Nada's and First Mother's creations. Metatron is a member of the Elohim and His reputation is legendary and formidable. An experience of my own with this level of the angelic realm is a lighter one, however.

Purity and Astrea are a Twin Flame pair of Elohim assigned to protect Brede and Jeshua. I knew about them for some time before I met them and meeting them was a surprise. They came to me as little girls, about seven years old with missing front teeth, dressed in what looked like children's Halloween costumes, white feather boa wings and all. When they informed me that they were our protectors, I asked, "But who's going to protect you?" "We're very aware," Purity said. And Astrea added, "We don't miss anything; nothing gets past us." They asked for a red ball to play with. I'm sure their appearances are deceiving, as the Elohim are known as some of the toughest warriors of the Light.

I have already discussed the **Presences of the Light**, but will do so here briefly again. They are genetic designers of life and the Light, creators of species, and keepers of Nada's eggs of creation. Nada is their Mother and they in turn are the Mothers of the angelic and other realms. Working at the Multi-Cosmic System level, they program and protect the Master Templates, the Creational Computers one step below the Master Light. Presences of the Light are Goddesses and Gods, as well as being the highest level of the angelic realm.

The **Creator Light Ships** operate on all levels, from the Earth through the Multi-Cosmic System. They contain the science and technologies of the Light, including the genetic technologies, as well as the Light's weaponry and defense, and they are the protectors of all of life. As keepers of the holograms and Particles of all sentient Be-ings, the Light Ships protect the Collectivity of the Light. They also transmit the Radiance of the Light Beyond the Goddesses, relaying the life force from First Mother to Earth and back again, and connecting the Above with the Below on all levels coming and going.

Also at the Multi-Cosmic System level, angelic realm Be-ings known as **Principals** or Principalities have the single-focused job of protecting the Master Light, the mainframe Creational Computers at First Mother's level. The Master Light is a living duplication of the Light Beyond.

At the Multi-Verse level, **Powers** are the angelic realm protectors of the highest level creators of the Light. These include Nada, First Mother, the First Sources of the Light, and the Ultimate Sources of the Light—and all they create.

Thrones work on the Infini-Verse level as protectors of the Light Beyond and of the Combined Ultimate Sources of the Light. They protect the Absolute Divinities and the pristine Solar source of Light itself. Their foremost job is to make sure that the Light, and the sources of the Light, are never invaded, corrupted or destroyed again.

The Light is diverse and varied, as are the Light Be-ings that comprise it. If the above discussion does not answer the questions presented at the start of this chapter, it begins to at least. The information offers more answers than what most people would think to ask for. The questions, "Who is God (or Goddess)?" and "Who made us?" have many answers. Which one is *the* answer is yet unknown. Of the questions, "Where did we come from?" and "Why were we made?", the material of this book so far offers more information than has ever before been known on Earth.

From here we begin the *Essential Energy Balancing III* processes. Doing the work of this book will bring you answers—and probably a lot more questions. Follow your heart and it will lead you to the truth.

Before You Begin

In *Essential Energy Balancing* you completed your requirement for Earth through Solar System incarnation. In *Essential Energy Balancing II* you completed your requirement for Galactic incarnation. With *Essential Energy Balancing III* most women will bring in a Goddess to join permanently with her energy, some men will bring in Gods, and a few of both will join with a Family of Light. In our original Creational Programming, ascension meant leaving our bodies behind. In this lifetime, however, we are not ready to leave but choose instead to bring the Goddess or God to live with us on Earth.

To accomplish and assure this, the following statements must be made before you go further.

1. Ask to speak with the Lords of Karma, Divine Director, and the Karmic Board.

2. Make the following statement:

    I request that my Creational Programming be revised to include the following:

    I ask that my ascension and all ascension processes be completed while in my body on Earth and that I remain alive and in my body after ascension for the period of my full incarnation.

    I also ask that I not end my incarnation on Earth with my ascension, but that I remain incarnated, with my Goddess's or God's full presence, until this lifetime is completed.

3. Ask for these things:

    Fully, completely, permanently and forever,

Through all the levels and components of your Be-ing,

All dimensions, all connections, all systems and between them,

Through all lifetimes and between them,

Of and between all dimensions of your multidimensional Be-ing, your Goddess's or God's Be-ing, your union, total union, and ascension.

Immediately and instantly,

Past, present and future,

NOW.

This is slightly different from the usual Short Process completion with Divine Director.

4. Wait for a response. No one will be refused, but you may be given further instructions. Follow the instructions.

5. Thank the Lords of Karma, Divine Director and the Karmic Board.

If you are bringing in a Goddess or God:

a) Make the above request for the Creational Programming of your Goddess or God.

b) Make the above request for the Creational Programming of your Goddess/God Union.

Also before you begin, if you haven't already done so, you must make the request to connect the full complement of your DNA. To do this, ask to speak with the Lords of Karma, Divine Director and the Karmic Board and phrase your request as follows:

I ask to clear, heal, reconnect and fully activate the full complement of my DNA.

You will perceive a "yes" or "no" response. If the response is "yes" no more is needed. If you are refused, ask what you need to do to have your DNA reconnected and restored, and follow the directions you are given. If you do not perceive a response, consider it a "yes" and know that the work is begun. Your request begins the reconnection, which is an ongoing process of at least several months.

From this point, you may begin the twenty-four processes of *Essential Energy Balancing III.*

The Processes

Process I Second Re-Creation and Reprogramming

YOUR CREATION IS AN ENERGY COMPONENT, A TYPE OF COMPUTER programming. This programming was compromised and damaged before the creation of the Earth by the Negative Greys and Orion, and the invader Chain of Evil. The first Re-Creation and Replacement Process (in *Essential Energy Balancing II* and repeated in Appendix I of this book) was done to remove the Source of All Evil from your and the Earth's Creation. This second process completes the removal of all evil from your energy and Creation and offers full protection from further mutation. Our Creation was made in total purity and perfection; this process asks to return that birthright to us.

1. Ask to speak with Divine Director, the Lords of Karma, and the Karmic Board. Ask them to REPLACE AND RE-CREATE THE PROGRAMMING OF YOUR COSMIC AND BEYOND COSMIC CREATION AND ALL YOUR ENERGY, adding to it total protection, shielding and healing for you (your Goddess or God, your union, total union and ascension) from The Source of All Evil and all its creations and manifestations, the Negative Greys, Orion, The Negative Form, the Goddesses' Evil Twins and all aspects and manifestations of evil and the Chain of Evil, including all attacks, all negative vows given and received, all curses and spells, all evil and negative use of energy, all mechanisms, weapons, damage, harm, obstructions and interference, and all their access to your

energy. Ask for complete and total protection, especially for your Galactic Cord system and all its components, transformers and connections, and for all connections to your Goddess or God, the Light and to the Earth.

2. Ask to REPLACE AND RE-CREATE THE PROGRAMMING OF YOUR COSMIC AND BEYOND COSMIC CREATION AND ALL YOUR ENERGY, to make your Creation and all your energy (and that of your Goddess or God, your union, total union and ascension) a self-healing, self-regenerating, self-replacing (as needed), self-protecting, self-defending, self-maintaining, self-opening, self-activating, self-clearing and self-purifying system.

3. Next ask that your new Cosmic and Beyond Cosmic Creational programming DELETE FROM YOUR CREATION AND ALL YOUR ENERGY AND YOUR LIFE (and that of your Goddess or God, your union, total union, and ascension) all suffering, agony, fear, abandonment, abuse, victimhood, anger and rage, grief, sorrow, aging, vengeance and viciousness, debilitation, dis-ease, pain, lack and need. Ask that your new Creational Programming and all your energy be brought back to the full purity, joy, total healing, protection, abundance, love, good health, family, community, harmony, grace, ease and peace they were meant to have.

4. Ask to REPLACE ALL COMPONENTS AND CONNECTIONS THROUGH ALL SYSTEMS THAT MANIFEST THE ABOVE DAMAGE OR EVIL AND RECONNECT ALL SYSTEMS TO TOTAL PURITY AND PERFECTION, TOTAL PROTECTION AND HEALING for you, your Goddess or God, your union, total union and ascension.

5. Ask that The Source of All Evil and all its creations and manifestations, the Negative Greys, Orion, The Negative Form, the Evil Twins and Evil Hybrids, the Chain of Evil and all the evils and negatives above be ANNIHILATED, EXTINGUISHED, UNCREATED AND OBLITERATED from your new Cosmic and Beyond

Cosmic Creational Programming and all your energy, and from your Goddess or God (your union, total union, and ascension), and from the Earth, all Be-ings, all life, and from the All.

6. Ask that your new Cosmic and Beyond Cosmic Creation and all your energy be programmed to CANCEL ALL KARMA AND ALL KARMIC CONTRACTS with the above deletions forever, with The Source of all Evil and all its creations and manifestations, the Negative Greys, Orion, The Negative Form, the Evil Twins and Hybrids, and with all the negatives and evils above. Ask to cancel all karma and all karmic contracts preventing the positives we have requested from fully manifesting for you, your Goddess or God, your union, total union, and ascension.

7. Ask to HEAL AND REGENERATE ALL DAMAGE to your Cosmic and Beyond Cosmic Creation and all your energy, replacing all components and connections that are too damaged to easily heal or that are carrying replication of evil. Ask for full reconnection of all energies, and for full and optimal function of all components, connections and systems. Ask for total safety and protection for your reprogrammed Creation, all your energy and all the positives above forever. Ask for the return of your absolute Creational purity and perfection, and the end of all replication of evil in your energy and your Cosmic and Beyond Cosmic Creation forever. Request all of these things for you, your Goddess or God, your union, total union, and ascension.

8. Request to TRANSFIGURE YOUR NEW COSMIC AND BEYOND COSMIC CREATION AND ALL YOUR ENERGY AGAINST THE SOURCE OF ALL EVIL AND ALL ITS CREATIONS AND MANIFESTATIONS FOREVER, INCLUDING THE NEGATIVE GREYS, ORION AND THE NEGATIVE FORM, THE CHAIN OF EVIL AND ALL THE DELETIONS ABOVE. Ask to TRANSFIGURE YOUR NEW COSMIC AND BEYOND COSMIC CREATION AND YOUR ENERGY FOR THE LIGHT FOREVER, and UNTO THE

LIGHT AND UNTO PROTECTION FOREVER for you, your Goddess or God, your union, total union, and ascension.

9. Ask for COSMIC AND BEYOND COSMIC KARMIC DISSOLUTION from all that prevents this total transfiguration or any of the requests above from being fulfilled.

10. Ask for all of these things in the name of the Light; on Earth and all other planets and between them, through all lifetimes and between them, through all dimensions and multidimensions and between them, of and between all dimensions of your multidimensional Be-ing (and that of your Goddess or God, your union, total union, and ascension).

11. Ask for these things fully, completely, permanently and forever, through all the levels and components of your Be-ing, all dimensions, all connections, all systems and between them, through all multidimensions and between them of your multidimensional Be-ing (and your Goddess or God, union, total union, and ascension).

12. Request these healings immediately and instantly under Karmic Law, past, present and future, forever and NOW.

13. Thank the Lords of Karma, Divine Director, the Karmic Board, and the Light.

Universal Healings These are important to do.

a) Repeat the full process above, but instead of doing it for *your* Cosmic and Beyond Cosmic Creation and energy, do it for ALL CREATION AND ALL ENERGY.

b) Do the full process above, wording it for THE COSMIC AND BEYOND COSMIC CREATION AND ENERGY OF YOUR GODDESS OR GOD, AND OF YOUR GODDESS/GOD UNION.

c) Do the full process above, wording it for THE COSMIC AND BEYOND COSMIC CREATION AND ENERGY OF ALL THE GODDESSES AND GODS, GODDESS/GOD

UNIONS, GREAT GODDESS/GOD UNIONS, AND ALL
BE-INGS AND REALMS OF THE LIGHT AS APPROPRI-
ATE AND NEEDED FOR EACH.

d) Repeat the process again, wording it for THE COSMIC
AND BEYOND COSMIC CREATION AND ENERGY OF
THE EARTH, ALL LIFE, ALL BE-INGS, ALL PLANETS,
AND FOR ALL OF THE ALL AS APPROPRIATE AND
NEEDED FOR EACH.

e) Repeat the process once more wording it for THE COSMIC
AND BEYOND COSMIC CREATION AND ENERGY OF
YOUR HOME, GARDEN, CAR, COMPUTER, BELONG-
INGS, PETS, AND CHILDREN. (Adults living in the home
must make the requests for themselves.)

Process II Sword, Chalice, Shield Fusion

IN *ESSENTIAL ENERGY BALANCING II* AND IN *RELIANCE ON THE LIGHT*, YOU WERE given the Sword, Chalice and Shield of Archangel Michael. This time, these articles of protection are to be installed in your Creational Programming—for you, your Goddess or God, and your union with Her or Him. They are also to be installed in your total union, your ascension, and in your Galactic Cord and Grounding Cord systems. The fusion, transfiguration and activation of these articles is the fusion, transfiguration and activation of your Goddess/God Union. As a number of protecting Archangels are now present for ascension candidates and their unions, I am replacing Archangel Michael's name with that of "your Dimensional Archangel."

1. Ask to speak with the Lords of Karma, Divine Director, your Dimensional Archangel, and the Karmic Board. Request the REPROGRAMMING OF YOUR CREATION TO INSTALL YOUR DIMENSIONAL ARCHANGEL'S SWORD OF PROTECTION AND TRUTH IN YOUR ENERGY, YOUR GODDESS'S OR GOD'S ENERGY, IN THE ENERGY OF YOUR UNION, IN YOUR TOTAL UNION AND ASCENSION, AND IN ALL GALACTIC CORD AND GROUNDING CORD SYSTEMS IN THEIR COMPLETELY SYNCHRONIZED AND COMPLEMENTARY STATE. The sword's use is to fight evil and protect the Light. If at this step or any other of the process, your request is denied, ask what you must do to have it, and follow the directions that will be given to you. Otherwise, continue.

2. If the request is granted, ask where the Sword is to be installed in each. There will be seven Swords, one in you, one in your Goddess or God, one in your union, one in your total union, one in your ascension, and one each in your Galactic Cord and Grounding Cord systems. They will be in seven different places.

If the request is granted, but you are not shown locations, you may still continue.

3. Ask that the reprogramming be completed and the Swords be installed.

4. Now REQUEST THE REPROGRAMMING OF YOUR CREATION TO INSTALL YOUR DIMENSIONAL ARCHANGEL'S KARMIC SHIELD IN YOUR ENERGY, YOUR GODDESS OR GOD'S ENERGY, IN THE ENERGY OF YOUR UNION, IN YOUR TOTAL UNION AND ASCENSION, AND IN ALL GALACTIC CORD AND GROUNDING CORD SYSTEMS IN THEIR COMPLETELY SYNCHRONIZED AND COMPLEMENTARY STATE. The Shield protects you from the return of old karma.

5. If the request is granted, ask where the Shield is to be installed in each. There will be seven Shields, one in you, one in your Goddess or God, one in your union, one in your total union, one in your ascension, and one each in your Galactic Cord and Grounding Cord systems. They will be in seven different places. If the request is granted, but you are not shown locations, you may still continue.

6. Ask that the reprogramming be completed and the Shields be installed.

7. Next, REQUEST THE REPROGRAMMING OF YOUR CREATION TO INSTALL YOUR DIMENSIONAL ARCHANGEL'S CHALICE OF HEALING AND REGENERATION IN YOUR ENERGY, YOUR GODDESS OR GOD'S ENERGY, IN THE ENERGY OF YOUR UNION, IN YOUR TOTAL UNION AND ASCENSION, AND IN ALL GALACTIC CORD AND GROUNDING CORD SYSTEMS IN THEIR COMPLETELY SYNCHRONIZED AND COMPLEMENTARY STATE. The Chalice's use is for the automatic self-healing of your energy.

8. If the request is granted, ask where the Chalice is to be installed in each. There will be seven Chalices, one in you, one in your Goddess or God, one in your union, one in your total union, one in your ascension, and one each in your Galactic Cord and Grounding Cord systems. They will be in seven different places. If the request is granted, but you are not shown locations, you may still continue.

9. Ask that the reprogramming be completed and the Chalices be installed.

10. Now ask for THE FULL REPROGRAMMING OF YOUR CRE-ATION FOR THE FULL, CONTINUOUS AND PERMANENT ACTIVATION OF THE SWORDS, SHIELDS AND CHALICES IN YOUR ENERGY, YOUR GODDESS OR GOD'S ENERGY, IN THE ENERGY OF YOUR UNION, TOTAL UNION AND ASCENSION, AND IN ALL GALACTIC CORD AND GROUNDING CORD SYS-TEMS FOREVER. Request the complete insulation of your energy to protect the full activations. Wait for this to be done; unless you receive a "no" response, its happening. Ask when to go on.

11. Request the full activation of the Swords, Shields and Chalices.

12. When all seven Swords, Shields and Chalices in you, your Goddess/God, your union, total union, ascension, and Galactic Cord and Grounding Cord systems are fully activated, request the following. Ask the Lords of Karma, Divine Director, the Karmic Board, and your Dimensional Archangel for THE FULL REPRO-GRAMMING OF YOUR CREATION TO MERGE AND FUSE, AND TO TRANSFIGURE THE MERGING AND FUSION OF THE SWORDS, CHALICES AND SHIELDS. The seven Swords will be fused together, the seven Shields will be fused together, and the seven Chalices will be fused together, thereby fusing you, your Goddess or God and your union, total union and ascension into one. Ask when the fusion and transfiguration are complete; wait for this before going on.

13. Ask the Lords of Karma, Divine Director, the Karmic Board, and your Dimensional Archangel for THE FULL REPROGRAMMING OF YOUR CREATION TO FULLY ACTIVATE THE FUSION AND TRANSFIGURATION OF THE SWORDS, SHIELDS AND CHALICES, AND THEREBY FULLY ACTIVATE AND TRANSFIGURE YOUR UNION WITH YOUR GODDESS OR GOD. Wait for this to complete.

14. To finish, ask for these healings and reprogrammings in the name of the Light: on Earth and all other planets and between them, through all lifetimes and between them, through all dimensions, multidimensions and between them, of and between all dimensions of you and your Goddess or God's multidimensional Be-ing, your union, total union, and ascension.

15. Ask for these things fully, completely, permanently and forever, through all the levels and components of your Be-ing, all dimensions, all connections, all systems and between them, through all multidimensions and between them of you, your Goddess or God, your union, total union, and ascension's multidimensional Be-ing.

16. Request these healings and reprogrammings immediately and instantly, past, present and future, forever and NOW.

17. Thank the Lords of Karma, Divine Director, the Karmic Board, and your Dimensional Archangel.

Universal Healings

a) Repeat the full process above, requesting it for ALL CREATION AND ALL ENERGY.

b) Do the full process above, wording it for the CREATION AND ENERGY OF YOUR GODDESS OR GOD, AND OF YOUR GODDESS/GOD UNION.

c) Do the full process above, wording it for THE CREATION AND ENERGY OF ALL THE GODDESSES AND GODS,

GODDESS/GOD UNIONS, GREAT GODDESS/GOD UNIONS, AND ALL BE-INGS OF THE LIGHT.

d) Repeat the process again, wording it for THE CREATION AND ENERGY OF THE EARTH, ALL LIFE, ALL BE-INGS, AND ALL PLANETS.

e) Repeat the process above, requesting THE REPROGRAM-MING OF YOUR CREATION AND ENERGY TO INSTALL YOUR DIMENSIONAL ARCHANGEL'S SWORD, SHIELD AND CHALICE IN YOUR HOME, GARDEN, CAR, COM-PUTER, BELONGINGS, PETS, AND CHILDREN. (Adults living in the home must make the requests for themselves.) Make sure the articles of protection are all installed and are fully and forever activated.

Process III Interdimensional Sword, Chalice and Shield

YOUR INTERDIMENSIONAL ARCHANGEL'S SWORDS, CHALICES AND SHIELDS protect you through the Galaxy's Interspace Grid, the spaces between the dimensions, where those of your Dimensional Archangel protect the dimensions of the Earth, Moon and Solar System. Added to your Dimensional Archangel's Swords, Chalices and Shields, those of your Interdimensional Archangel complete the total protections needed for the safety of your Goddess or God on Earth. Archangel Ashtar is the keeper of the Galaxy's interspace grid, but He is no longer the only Interdimensional protector for Goddess or God Unions.

You will note that as in the previous process there are seven Swords and Chalices. Here, however, there are eight (instead of seven) Shields. The additional Shield, the fusion of the combined protections, is provided by Archangel Metatron. It extends the protection and healing to and through the dimensions and interdimensions of our Universe.

1. Ask to speak with the Lords of Karma, Divine Director, your Dimensional Archangel, your Interdimensional Archangel, Metatron, and the Karmic Board. Request the REPROGRAM-MING OF YOUR CREATION TO INSTALL YOUR INTERDI-MENSIONAL ARCHANGEL'S SWORD OF PROTECTION AND TRUTH IN YOUR ENERGY, YOUR GODDESS'S OR GOD'S ENERGY, IN THE ENERGY OF YOUR UNION, IN YOUR TOTAL UNION AND ASCENSION, AND IN ALL GALACTIC CORD AND GROUNDING CORD SYSTEMS IN THEIR COMPLETELY SYNCHRONIZED AND COMPLEMENTARY STATE. The Sword's use is to fight evil between the dimensions. If at this step or any other of the process, your request is denied, ask what you must do to have it and follow the directions that will be given to you. Otherwise continue.

2. If the request is granted, ask where the Sword is to be installed in each. There will be seven Swords, one in you, one in your Goddess or God, one in your union, one in your total union, one in your ascension, and one each in your Galactic Cord and Grounding Cord systems. They will be in seven different places. If the request is granted, but you are not shown locations, you may still continue.

3. Ask that the reprogramming be completed and the Swords be installed.

4. Now REQUEST THE REPROGRAMMING OF YOUR CREATION TO INSTALL YOUR INTERDIMENSIONAL ARCHANGEL'S KARMIC SHIELD IN YOUR ENERGY, YOUR GODDESS'S OR GOD'S ENERGY, IN THE ENERGY OF YOUR UNION, IN YOUR TOTAL UNION AND ASCENSION, AND IN ALL GALACTIC CORD AND GROUNDING CORD SYSTEMS IN THEIR COMPLETELY SYNCHRONIZED AND COMPLEMENTARY STATE. There is one further shield—that of Archangel Metatron's fusion of your combined Dimensional and Interdimensional protections—to make a total of eight levels. The Shield protects you from the return of old interplanetary karma.

5. If the request is granted, ask where the Shield is to be installed in each. There will be seven Shields, one in you, one in your Goddess or God, one in your union, one in your total union, one in your ascension, and one each in your Galactic Cord and Grounding Cord systems. If you see the eighth, it will be surrounding all the others at the end of this process. The seven Shields will be in seven different places. If the request is granted, but you are not shown locations, continue.

6. Ask that the reprogramming be completed and the Shields be installed.

7. Next, REQUEST THE REPROGRAMMING OF YOUR CREATION TO INSTALL YOUR INTERDIMENSIONAL ARCHANGEL'S

CHALICE OF HEALING AND REGENERATION IN YOUR ENERGY, YOUR GODDESS'S OR GOD'S ENERGY, IN THE ENERGY OF YOUR UNION, IN YOUR TOTAL UNION AND ASCENSION, AND IN ALL GALACTIC CORD AND GROUNDING CORD SYSTEMS IN THEIR COMPLETELY SYNCHRONIZED AND COMPLEMENTARY STATE. The Chalice's use is for automatic self-healing in the spaces between dimensions.

8. If the request is granted, ask where the Chalice is to be installed in each. There will be seven Chalices, one in you, one in your Goddess or God, one in your union, one in your total union, one in your ascension, and one each in your Galactic Cord and Grounding Cord systems. They will be in seven different places. If the request is granted, but you are not shown locations, you may still continue.

9. Ask that the reprogramming be completed and the Chalices be installed.

10. Now ask for THE FULL REPROGRAMMING OF YOUR CREATION FOR THE FULL, CONTINUOUS AND PERMANENT ACTIVATION OF THE SWORDS, SHIELDS AND CHALICES IN YOUR ENERGY, YOUR GODDESS'S OR GOD'S ENERGY, IN THE ENERGY OF YOUR UNION, TOTAL UNION AND ASCENSION, AND IN ALL GALACTIC CORD AND GROUNDING CORD SYSTEMS FOREVER. Request the complete insulation of your energy to protect the full activations. Wait for this to be done; unless you receive a "no" response, its happening. Ask when to go on.

11. Request the full activation of your Interdimensional Archangel's Swords, Shields and Chalices.

12. When all seven Swords, eight Shields and seven Chalices in you, your Goddess or God, your union, total union and ascension, and all Galactic Cord and Grounding Cord systems are fully activated, request the following. Ask the Lords of Karma, Divine Director, the

Karmic Board, your Dimensional and Interdimensional Archangels, and Archangel Metatron for THE FULL REPRO-GRAMMING OF YOUR CREATION TO MERGE AND FUSE, AND TO TRANSFIGURE THE MERGING AND FUSION OF THE SWORDS, SHIELDS AND CHALICES. The seven Swords will be fused together, the eight Shields will be fused together, and the seven Chalices will be fused together. Ask when the fusion and transfiguration are complete; wait for this before going on.

13. Ask the Lords of Karma, Divine Director, the Karmic Board, your Dimensional and Interdimensional Archangels, and Archangel Metatron for the FULL REPROGRAMMING OF YOUR CRE-ATION TO FULLY ACTIVATE THE FUSION AND TRANSFIGU-RATION OF THE SWORDS, SHIELDS AND CHALICES, AND THEREBY FULLY ACTIVATE AND TRANSFIGURE THE INTER-DIMENSIONAL PROTECTION OF YOUR UNION WITH YOUR GODDESS OR GOD. Wait for this to complete.

14. Now ask the Lords of Karma, Divine Director, the Karmic Board, your Dimensional Archangel, Interdimensional Archangel, and Archangel Metatron for the FULL REPROGRAMMING OF YOUR CREATION TO MERGE AND FUSE, AND TO TRANSFIGURE THE MERGING AND FUSION OF YOUR INTERDIMENSIONAL ARCHANGEL'S SWORDS, SHIELDS AND CHALICES WITH THOSE OF YOUR DIMENSIONAL ARCHANGEL. Wait for this to be done; unless you receive a "no" response, it's happening. Ask when to go on.

15. Ask the Lords of Karma, Divine Director, the Karmic Board, your Dimensional and Interdimensional Archangels, and Archangel Metatron for the FULL REPROGRAMMING OF YOUR CREATION TO FULLY ACTIVATE THE FUSION AND TRANSFIGURATION OF THE COMBINED SWORDS, SHIELDS AND CHALICES OF YOUR INTERDIMENSIONAL AND DIMENSIONAL ARCH-ANGELS, AND THEREBY FULLY ACTIVATE AND TRANSFIGURE

YOUR UNION WITH YOUR GODDESS OR GOD. Request also to FULLY ACTIVATE AND TRANSFIGURE THE TOTAL PROTEC-TION OF YOU, YOUR GODDESS OR GOD, YOUR UNION, TOTAL UNION AND ASCENSION, AND ALL GALACTIC CORD AND GROUNDING CORD SYSTEMS IN THEIR COMPLETELY SYNCHRONIZED AND COMPLEMENTARY STATE. Ask for the complete insulation of your energy to protect the full activation and transfiguration. Wait for this to complete.

16. To finish, ask for these healings and reprogrammings in the name of the Light: on Earth and all other planets and between them, through all lifetimes and between them, through all dimensions, multidimensions and between them, of and between all dimensions of you and your Goddess's or God's multidimensional Be-ing, union, total union, and ascension.

17. Ask for these things fully, completely, permanently and forever, through all the levels and components of your Be-ing, all dimensions, all connections, all systems and between them, through all multidimensions and between them, of you, your Goddess or God, your union, total union, and ascension's multidimensional Be-ing.

18. Request these healings and reprogrammings immediately and instantly, past, present and future, forever and NOW.

19. Thank the Lords of Karma, Divine Director, the Karmic Board, your Dimensional and Interdimensional Archangels, and Archangel Metatron.

Universal Healings

a) Repeat the full process above, but instead of doing it for *your* Creation and energy, do it for ALL CREATION AND ALL ENERGY.

b) Do the full process above, wording it for THE CREATION AND ENERGY OF YOUR GODDESS OR GOD, AND OF YOUR GODDESS/GOD UNION.

c) Do the full process above, wording it for THE CREATION AND ENERGY OF ALL THE GODDESSES AND GODS, GODDESS/GOD UNIONS, GREAT GODDESS/GOD UNIONS, AND ALL BE-INGS OF THE LIGHT.

d) Repeat the process again, wording it for THE CREATION AND ENERGY OF THE EARTH, MOON, SOLAR SYSTEM, GALAXY, UNIVERSE, COSMOS AND BEYOND, ALL LIFE, ALL BE-INGS AND ALL THE LIGHT.

e) Do the full process again, wording it for THE CREATION AND ENERGY OF ALL PLANETARY GRIDS AND STRUCTURES, INCLUDING THE WELL OF LIFE AND FIRE OF LIFE AT THE CENTER OF THE EARTH AND ALL PLANETS, AND THE PLANETARY CORE.

f) Repeat the process once more, requesting THE REPROGRAMMING OF YOUR CREATION AND ENERGY TO INSTALL YOUR INTERDIMENSIONAL ARCHANGEL'S AND METATRON'S SWORD, SHIELD AND CHALICE IN YOUR HOME, GARDEN, CAR, COMPUTER, BELONGINGS, PETS, AND CHILDREN. (Adults living in the home must make the requests for themselves.) Make sure the articles of interspace protection are all installed and are fully and forever activated.

Process IV   Creational Energy Balancing

THIS PROCESS IS THE WAY TO BRING ALL ENERGY SYSTEMS INTO PERMANENT dynamic balance and clearing. I have sought the means for this since the start of the Essential Energy Balancing system, and the key is Creational Repatterning. Once you have made the request, the process takes twenty-four hours to complete; it is best done in bed at night, the last thing before sleep.

1. Ask to speak with the Lords of Karma, Divine Director, and the Karmic Board.

2. Request the FULL REPROGRAMMING OF YOUR COSMIC AND BEYOND COSMIC CREATION FOR COMPLETE, PERMANENT AND FOREVER ESSENTIAL ENERGY BALANCING AND CLEARING THROUGH ALL SYSTEMS for you, your Goddess or God, your union, total union, and ascension.

3. Also request the FULL REPROGRAMMING OF YOUR COSMIC AND BEYOND COSMIC CREATION TO FULLY SYNCHRONIZE AND MATCH YOUR ENERGY WITH THAT OF YOUR GOD-DESS OR GOD.

4. Ask for these healings and reprogrammings in the name of the Light: on Earth and all other planets and between them, through all lifetimes and between them, through all dimensions, multidi-mensions and between them, of and between all dimensions of you and your Goddess's or God's multidimensional Be-ing, your union, total union, and ascension.

5. Ask for these things fully, completely, permanently and forever, through all the levels and components of your Be-ing, all dimen-sions, all connections, all systems and between them, through all multidimensions and between them of you, your Goddess or God, your union, total union, and ascension's multidimensional Be-ing.

6. Request these healings and reprogrammings immediately and instantly, past, present and future, forever and NOW.

7. Thank the Lords of Karma, Divine Director, and the Karmic Board.

Universal Healings

a) Request the full Cosmic and Beyond Cosmic Creational Reprogramming above for your HOME, GARDEN, CAR, COMPUTER, BELONGINGS, PETS, AND CHILDREN.

Process V Cancellation of Karmic Contracts

KARMIC CONTRACTS ARE INHERENTLY NEGATIVE—ALL OF THEM. THIS PROCESS ends all karmic contracts from all lifetimes. It is as important to do this for your Goddess or God as it is for yourself.

1. Ask to speak with the Lords of Karma, Divine Director, and the Karmic Board.

2. Ask to CANCEL ALL KARMA AND ALL KARMIC CONTRACTS WITH ALL PAST LIVES AND ALL PAST INCARNATIONS for you, your Goddess or God, your union, total union, and ascension.

3. Request also to CANCEL ALL KARMA AND ALL KARMIC CONTRACTS FOR THIS LIFE AND THIS INCARNATION for you, your Goddess or God, your union, total union and ascension.

4. Ask for these things on Earth and all other planets and between them, through all lifetimes and between them, through all dimensions, multidimensions and between them, of and between all dimensions of you and your Goddess or God, your union, total union, and ascension's multidimensional Be-ing.

5. Request these things fully, completely, permanently and forever, through all the levels and components of your Be-ing, all dimensions, all connections, all systems and between them, through all multidimensions and between them of you, your Goddess or God, your union, total union, and ascension's multidimensional Be-ing.

6. Request these healings immediately and instantly, past, present and future, forever and NOW.

7. Thank the Lords of Karma, Divine Director, and the Karmic Board.

Universal Healings

a) Request the above for ALL GODDESS/GOD UNIONS, TOTAL UNIONS, AND ASCENSIONS.

Process VI   DNA Repatterning

DAMAGE, DIS-EASE AND SOME ATTACKS ARE REPLICATED—PROGRAMMED INTO your energy—through the DNA by way of your Creation. This process is to clear your DNA and your Cosmic and Beyond Cosmic Creational Programming of all such negative and evil replications and to heal all energy damage derived from them. This damage can come from any life-time or between life state on Earth or other planets in any cosmos.

1. Ask to speak with the Lords of Karma, Divine Director, the Karmic Board, and Archangels Michael, Ashtar and Metatron.

2. Ask for the FULL REPROGRAMMING OF YOUR COSMIC AND BEYOND COSMIC CREATION FOR KARMIC DISSOLUTION FROM ALL SOURCES OF THE REPLICATION OF EVIL, attacks, negative vows and curses, obstructions, damage, dis-ease and malfunction from your DNA and all energy systems, for you, your Goddess or God, your union, total union, and ascension.

3. Request the FULL REPROGRAMMING OF YOUR COSMIC AND BEYOND COSMIC CREATION TO ANNIHILATE, EXTIN-GUISH, UNCREATE AND OBLITERATE from your DNA and all your energy all evil, attacks, negative vows and curses, obstruc-tions, damage, dis-ease, despair, malfunction and their replica-tion from all sources for you, your Goddess or God, your union, total union, and ascension.

4. Request the FULL REPROGRAMMING OF YOUR COSMIC AND BEYOND COSMIC CREATION FOR TOTAL PURIFICATION OF YOUR DNA AND ALL YOUR ENERGY, returning them to the absolutely pure and pristine state that they were meant to have, for you, your Goddess or God, your union, total union, and ascension.

5. Ask for the FULL REPROGRAMMING OF YOUR COSMIC AND BEYOND COSMIC CREATION FOR TOTAL HEALING AND

REGENERATION OF YOUR DNA AND ALL YOUR ENERGY, including replacement of all components or connections that are too damaged to readily heal, that are missing, or that were carrying replication of the negatives and evils listed above. Ask for the full reprogramming of your Cosmic and Beyond Cosmic Creation to include total reconnection, all systems brought back to full and optimal function, and full, permanent and continuous activation and opening for you, your Goddess or God, your union, total union, and ascension.

6. Request the FULL REPROGRAMMING OF YOUR COSMIC AND BEYOND COSMIC CREATION FOR TOTAL SAFETY AND PROTECTION, with all protections fully installed, merged, fused, transfigured and activated. Ask for these things for you, your Goddess or God, your union, total union, and ascension.

7. Ask for these healings and reprogrammings in the name of the Light: on Earth and all other planets and between them, through all lifetimes and between them, through all dimensions, multidimensions and between them, of and between all dimensions of you and your Goddess's or God's multidimensional Be-ing, union, total union, and ascension.

8. Ask for these things fully, completely, permanently and forever, through all the levels and components of your Be-ing, all dimensions, all connections, all systems and between them, through all multidimensions and between them of you, your Goddess or God, your union, total union, and ascension's multidimensional Be-ing.

9. Request these healings and reprogrammings immediately and instantly, past, present and future, forever and NOW.

10. Thank the Lords of Karma, Divine Director, the Karmic Board, and Archangels Michael, Ashtar and Metatron.

Process VII   Planetary Healing

FROM THE VERY BEGINNING OF WORKING WITH THE LORDS OF KARMA, I HAVE sought for effective methods of planetary healing. Earth is in a dire state and the clear and present danger becomes more apparent with each passing day. The process that follows is a way to heal the Earth, though certainly not the only way. Note that instead of requesting the healings for your Creation, you ask it for Earth Creation instead. This first example is for cancelling negative and evil affirmations—from "I can't" or "you can't" to deliberate psychic attacks. It asks to end all negative and evil thinking, including self-directed negativity as well as harm and evil directed at you by others.

1. Ask to speak with the Lords of Karma, Divine Director, and the Karmic Board.

2. Request the FULL REPROGRAMMING OF EARTH CREATION TO CLEAR ALL NEGATIVE AND EVIL AFFIRMATIONS AND THEIR REPLICATION from all Creation, all DNA, and all energy for you, your Goddess or God, your union, total union and ascension, for the Earth, all Be-ings, and all life.

3. Request the FULL REPROGRAMMING OF EARTH CREATION TO ANNIHILATE, EXTINGUISH, UNCREATE AND OBLITER-ATE all sources of negative and evil affirmations from within and without, all negative and evil affirmations, their replications and all negative and evil effects, from all Creation, all DNA and all energy. Ask for these things for you, your Goddess or God, your union, total union and ascension, for the Earth, all Be-ings, and all life.

4. Request the FULL REPROGRAMMING OF EARTH CREATION FOR TOTAL PURIFICATION of all negative and evil affirmations and their replications from all Creation, all DNA and all energy, returning Earth and all Creation to the totally purified state it was

meant to have, for you, your Goddess or God, your union, total union and ascension, for the Earth, all Be-ings, and all life.

5. Ask for the FULL REPROGRAMMING OF EARTH CREATION FOR TOTAL HEALING AND REGENERATION of all damage from negative and evil affirmations for all Creation, all DNA and all energy, including replacement of all components or connections too damaged to readily heal, that are missing, or that were carrying replication of the negatives, evil and damage listed above. Ask for the full reprogramming of Earth Creation to include total reconnection, all systems returned to full and optimal function, and full, permanent and continuous activation and opening for you, your Goddess or God, your union, total union and ascension, for the Earth, all Be-ings, and all life.

6. Request the FULL REPROGRAMMING OF EARTH CREATION FOR TOTAL SAFETY AND PROTECTION, with all protections fully installed, merged, fused, transfigured and activated. Ask for these things for you, your Goddess or God, your union, total union, and ascension, for the Earth, all Be-ings, and all life.

7. Ask for these healings and reprogrammings in the name of the Light: on Earth and all other planets and between them, through all lifetimes and between them, through all dimensions, multidimensions and between them, of and between all dimensions of the Earth's multidimensional Be-ing, and of you, your Goddess or God, your union, total union, and ascension's multidimensional Be-ing, all Be-ings, and all life.

8. Ask for these things fully, completely, permanently and forever, through all the levels and components of Earth's Be-ing, all dimensions, all connections, all systems and between them, through all multidimensions and between them of all multidimensional Be-ings, unions, total unions, and ascensions.

9. Request these healings and reprogrammings immediately and instantly, past, present and future, forever and NOW.

10. Thank the Lords of Karma, Divine Director, and the Karmic Board.

Universal Healings

a) Use the complete process above to request the full reprogramming of Earth Creation to clear at the source ALL PLANETARY DAMAGE RESULTING IN CANCER, AIDS, CHRONIC FATIGUE AND ALL OTHER IMBALANCES OF NEGATIVE VIRUSES.

b) Use the complete process above to request the full reprogramming of Earth Creation to clear at the source ALL PLANETARY DAMAGE RESULTING IN THE DESTRUCTION OF THE OZONE LAYER and all its negative and evil effects on the planet, all Be-ings, and all life.

c) Repeat the process to request the full reprogramming of Earth Creation to clear all sources of PLANETARY DAMAGE RESULTING IN DESTRUCTIVE WEATHER PATTERNS and all their negative and evil effects on the planet, all Be-ings and all life. (These include such things as droughts, floods, hurricanes, wildfires, earthquakes, tornados, etc.)

d) The possibilities are endless.

Process VIII   DNA Transfiguration

ANOTHER NAME FOR THE NEGATIVE FORM IS EVIL DUALITY, THE AUTOMATIC pairing and twinning on every level of all good with evil. Evil Duality was programmed into Earth DNA by invader attacks on the Light Beyond, the Master Light, Earth's Creational Computers, and the Creational Computers of every structural level. This is the process to end all creation and replication of Evil Duality at its activational source point. It pulls the plug or flips the off-switch on the creation and activation of paired evil that blights all that is the Light. This work has already been completed on all levels but ours, and the clearing of the Earth is nearly finished.

1. Ask to speak with the Lords of Karma, Divine Director, the Karmic Board, Light Mother, Nada, St. Germaine, and Archangels Ashtar and Michael.

2. Request the FULL REPROGRAMMING OF EARTH CREATION AND PLANETARY DNA TO CANCEL ALL KARMA AND ALL KARMIC CONTRACTS AT THE SOURCE POINT WITH EVIL AND EVIL DUALITY'S CORRUPTION OF EARTH'S PURITY. Ask to cancel all karma and all karmic contracts with the creation, replication, regeneration, multiplication, and the switching-on or activation of NEGATIVE AND EVIL DNA that creates Evil Duality and all evil.

3. Ask for the FULL REPROGRAMMING OF EARTH CREATION AND PLANETARY DNA TO ANNIHILATE, EXTINGUISH, UNCREATE AND OBLITERATE ALL CORRUPTED DNA AND ITS CREATION, REPLICATION, REGENERATION, MULTIPLI-CATION, AND ACTIVATION FROM EARTH CREATION, EARTH DNA, ALL THE GODDESSES AND GODS, ALL PEOPLE, ALL BE-INGS AND ALL LIFE. Ask to annihilate, extinguish, uncreate and obliterate the Fallen Angels, the Negative Form Dualities of the Goddesses, and all Chains of Evil and their members.

4. Ask for the FULL REPROGRAMMING OF EARTH CREATION AND PLANETARY DNA FOR TOTAL PURIFICATION OF ALL CREATION AND ALL DNA FROM ALL EVIL DUALITY AND ALL EVIL, and total purification of all replication, regeneration, multiplication and activation of duality and evil from all DNA for all Earth Creation, Earth DNA, all the Goddesses and Gods, all Be-ings, and all life.

5. Request the FULL REPROGRAMMING OF EARTH CREATION AND PLANETARY DNA FOR TOTAL HEALING AND REGEN-ERATION OF EARTH CREATION AND POSITIVE DNA, includ-ing replacement of all components or connections too damaged to readily heal, that are missing, or that were carrying Negative Form Duality or the negatives, evil and damage listed above. Ask for the full reprogramming of Earth Creation and planetary DNA to include total reconnection of positive DNA, all systems returned to full and optimal function, and full, permanent and continuous positive activation and opening for all Earth Creation, Earth DNA, all the Goddesses and Gods, all Be-ings, and all life.

6. Request the FULL REPROGRAMMING OF EARTH CREATION AND PLANETARY DNA FOR TOTAL SAFETY AND PROTEC-TION—Archangel Michael's and Archangel Ashtar's Swords, Chalices and Shields installed, merged, fused and transfigured in dynamic function and activation forever.

7. Ask for the FULL REPROGRAMMING OF EARTH CREATION AND PLANETARY DNA TO TRANSFIGURE THEM AGAINST ALL EVIL DUALITY, ALL EVIL, ALL CORRUPTION, AND ALL REPLICATION, REGENERATION, MULTIPLICATION OR ACTI-VATION OF EVIL DUALITY FOREVER. Ask to transfigure Earth Creation and planetary DNA for the Light forever, and unto the Light and unto Protection forever.

8. Ask for these healings and reprogrammings in the name of the Light: on Earth and all other planets and between them, through

all lifetimes and between them, through all dimensions, multidimensions and between them, of and between all dimensions of the Earth and Earth DNA's multidimensional Be-ing. Ask for these healings and reprogrammings for YOU, YOUR GODDESS OR GOD, YOUR UNION, TOTAL UNION AND ASCENSION, for all the Goddesses and Gods, all Goddess/God Unions, all Be-ings, and all life.

9. Ask for these things fully, completely, permanently and forever, through all the levels and components of Earth's Be-ing, all dimensions, all connections, all systems and between them, through all multidimensions and between them, of and between the Earth and Earth DNA's multidimensional Be-ing. Ask for them for YOU, YOUR GODDESS OR GOD, YOUR UNION, TOTAL UNION AND ASCENSION, for all the Goddesses and Gods, all Goddess/God Unions, all Be-ings, and all life.

10. Request these healings and reprogrammings immediately and instantly, past, present and future, forever and NOW.

11. Thank the Lords of Karma, Divine Director, the Karmic Board, Light Mother, Nada, St. Germaine, and Archangels Michael and Ashtar.

12. Know that it is done.

Universal Healings

a) Request the full process above for YOU, YOUR GODDESS OR GOD, YOUR UNION, TOTAL UNION, AND ASCENSION, including all Galactic Cord and Grounding Cord systems.

b) Request the complete process above for ALL GODDESS/GOD UNIONS, TOTAL UNIONS AND ASCENSIONS, including all Galactic Cord and Grounding Cord systems, all Great Goddess/God Unions, and for the return of the Light to Earth.

Process IX To Bring in a Goddess or God

THE FOLLOWING IS A SUMMARY LIST OF WHAT IS NEEDED TO BRING IN YOUR Goddess or God. Most unions are Goddess Unions at this time, as only a few men have been permitted to bring in the Light so far. Women bring in Goddesses; men bring in Gods. Permission is required of the Lords of Karma, Divine Director and your Goddess or God. With that given, the following processes must be completed, using the exact wording given below. If you receive a "no" to any request, ask what is needed to release the no and follow instructions, or ask to cancel all karma and all karmic contracts from Earth and all other planets, all lifetimes and between them, that may be the source of the no.

See Appendix I at the end of this book for the full texts of all of the processes and requests needed, provided in proper sequence.

1. You must complete in order all the processes from *Essential Energy Balancing*.

2. Request of the Lords of Karma and Divine Director to clear, heal, reconnect, and fully activate the full compliment of your DNA. (Only a "yes" is needed here, no process is required.)

3. Request of the Lords of Karma and Divine Director that you bring in your Goddess or God to fully merge with you and live with you on Earth. Ask who the Goddess or God you will bring in is. Ask to cancel all karma and all karmic contracts from Earth and all other planets, from all lifetimes and between them, preventing you from bringing your Goddess or God in. (No process is required, only a "yes." If you are refused, you must accept the no.)

4. Ask the Lords of Karma and Divine Director to fully develop, establish, activate and open all Galactic Cord, Grounding Cord and Chain of Light components, systems and connections for you, your Goddess or God, your union, total union, and ascen-

sion. Use the Off Planet Karmic Release Process (the Short Process below) with the exact wording as follows. Use this process for all other karmic requests, as well.

SHORT PROCESS

Ask to speak with the Lords of Karma and Divine Director.

Make the request for you, your Goddess or God, your union, total union, and ascension, on Earth, all other planets and between them, through all lifetimes and between them, through all dimensions and multidimensions and between them, of and between all dimensions of your multidimensional Be-ing.

Ask for these things fully, completely, permanently and forever, through all the levels and components of your Be-ing, all dimensions, all connections, all systems, and between them, through all multidimensions and between them, of and between all dimensions of you, your Goddess or God, your union, total union, and ascension's multidimensional Be-ing.

Ask for these things immediately and instantly, past, present and future, forever and NOW.

Thank the Lords of Karma and Divine Director.

---

5. Request the full and complete healing of your Goddess or God, and to cancel all karma and all karmic contracts from all planets, lifetimes and between them, through all dimensions, multidimensions and between them, that could prevent Her (or His) total healing. (No process is required here, only a "yes." Use the above precise wording. If you are shown what needs healing, use the Short Process to request that it be done.)

6. Ask to cancel ALL karma and ALL karmic contracts from all lifetimes and incarnations on all planets and between them, including for this lifetime, for you, your Goddess or God, your union, total union, and ascension, past, present and future, forever and NOW. (No process is needed here, only a "yes.")

7. Do *Essential Energy Balancing II* Process XVIII—RE-CREATION AND REPLACEMENT. (Reprinted in Appendix I at the end of this book.)

8. Do *Essential Energy Balancing III* Process II—SWORD, CHALICE, SHIELD FUSION, and Process III—INTERDIMENSIONAL SWORD, CHALICE AND SHIELD. (Both are previous processes in this book; they also reprinted in Appendix I.)

No more is needed.

Process X The Violet Flame

THE VIOLET FLAME OF ST. GERMAINE IS THE MEANS TO PURIFY THE EARTH AND all Be-ings of Negative Form Duality and prevent its replication, regeneration, multiplication, reactivation, and its return. It also protects and clears the planet and the Goddess and God Unions from interference by Orion, Negative Grays and all Chain of Evil entities. The Violet Flame needs to be installed as a Creational Reprogramming permanently and forever around the Earth and around all Goddess/God Unions.

1. Ask to speak with the Lords of Karma, Divine Director, the Karmic Board, St. Germaine, and your Dimensional and Interdimensional Archangels.

2. Request the FULL REPROGRAMMING OF EARTH CREATION AND PLANETARY DNA TO INSTALL AND FULLY ACTIVATE THE VIOLET FLAME OF ST. GERMAINE IN AND AROUND THE EARTH AND ALL GODDESS/GOD UNIONS permanently and forever.

3. Request the FULL REPROGRAMMING OF EARTH CREATION AND PLANETARY DNA TO CANCEL ALL KARMA AND ALL KARMIC CONTRACTS AT THE SOURCE FOR THE EARTH AND ALL GODDESS/GOD UNIONS PREVENTING THIS PROTECTION, from Earth and all other planets, all lifetimes and incarnations, and between them.

4. Ask that the VIOLET FLAME BE INSTALLED AND FULLY AND FOREVER ACTIVATED NOW, in a Belt of Light surrounding the Earth, in and through all planetary grids and all structures, in the Well of Life and Fire of Life at the Center of the Earth, and in the planetary core. Ask that the Violet Flame be installed and fully and forever activated in a Belt of Light surrounding all Goddess/God Unions, and in and through them, immediately and forever.

5. Request the FULL REPROGRAMMING OF EARTH CREATION AND PLANETARY DNA FOR TOTAL PURIFICATION OF ALL NEGATIVE FORM DUALITY AND EVIL, and total purification of all replication, regeneration, multiplication, activation and return of Evil Duality and all evil from all Creation and all DNA for the Earth and all Goddess/God Unions, for all Be-ings, and all life.

6. Ask for these healings and reprogrammings in the name of the Light: on Earth and all other planets and between them, through all lifetimes and between them, through all dimensions, multidimensions and between them, of and between all dimensions of the Earth's and all Goddess/God Unions' multidimensional Be-ings. Ask for them, also for you, your Goddess or God, your union, total union, and ascension, for all Be-ings, and all life.

7. Ask for these things fully, completely, permanently and forever, through all the levels and components of all Be-ings, all dimensions, all connections, all systems and between them, through all multidimensions and between them, of and between all dimensions of the Earth's and all Goddess/God Unions' multidimensional Be-ings.

8. Request these healings and reprogrammings immediately and instantly, past, present and future, forever and NOW.

9. Thank the Lords of Karma, Divine Director, the Karmic Board, St. Germaine, and your Dimensional and Interdimensional Archangels.

Process XI Healing Others

I HAVE BEEN ASKED FREQUENTLY HOW TO MAKE DIVINE DIRECTOR REQUESTS FOR the healing of physical, emotional and mental dis-eases. Until now, almost all karmic healing could be done only for yourself. This is the way to use Divine Director's help for healing yourself, and for healing people or animals other than yourself, as well. You do not need to know the person you are requesting healing for, but you do need to know as precisely as possible what is wrong with them. You do not need the person's participation or permission for these healings, only Divine Director's. You will not be permitted to violate others' free will or karma.

It is necessary to use the exact wording and format below. If you receive a "no" make sure that you have asked for enough; you may talk with Divine Director about what is needed. If you are told that your request for others is inappropriate, you must stop immediately.

These healings are virtually instantaneous and they save lives. That we are granted Divine Director's help for healing others is a great gift given only to those who have surpassed both Earth and Galactic ascension. Use it very carefully, but use it at every presented opportunity to help others in service to the Light. Do not hesitate to use it to request healing for yourself.

1. Ask to speak with Divine Director.

2. Request to CLEAR, HEAL, RECONNECT AND FULLY ACTIVATE the full complement of the person to be healed's DNA.

3. Then, make the request for healing as follows:
   I ask for KARMIC DISSOLUTION at the source for (name) with (the issue or dis-ease) and all of its negative and evil effects. I ask for this release immediately, instantly and forever.

4. If the person you are healing is on the ascension path, as you are, replace the phrase "Karmic Dissolution" with "Cosmic and Beyond Cosmic Karmic Dissolution."

5. If you or the person you are healing is bringing in or has brought in a Goddess or God, word the request for the person, her or his Goddess or God, their union, total union, and ascension. Use the phrase "Cosmic and Beyond Cosmic Karmic Dissolution" in your request.

6. If the request is granted, next ask if there are any energies to ANNIHILATE, EXTINGUISH, UNCREATE AND OBLITERATE to achieve the full healing. If yes, request it; if no, go on.

7. Then ask if purification is needed, and if it is, request full and complete PURIFICATION of all energies, including the DNA and Creation as needed. If no purification is required, go to the next step.

8. Next, ask for total HEALING AND REGENERATION, with all components and connections replaced as needed, full reconnection, and full and optimal function and opening through all systems.

9. Ask for complete and total PROTECTION AND SAFETY for you or the person you are healing forever. No response to this is needed.

10. Ask if further requests are needed for full healing. You will either know what these requests are or you may ask Divine Director for guidance. Ask to add them to the above requests.

11. Thank Divine Director and know that it is done.

Process XII Karmic Dissolution

In *Essential Energy Balancing*, you requested karmic release or karmic severance to end karma from this or any other lifetime on Earth. In *Essential Energy Balancing II*, and until this time, the request has been for the cancellation of all karma and all karmic contracts with a person or issue to clear Galactic karma. Beyond our Galaxy is the Universe and Cosmos (and more). Our core souls—and our Goddesses or Gods who are the highest expressions of our core souls—were created far beyond the Cosmos. In our countless lifetimes, and our Goddesses' and Gods' countless lifetimes, remaining karma may exist beyond the Galaxy. The process of releasing this remaining karma is called Karmic Dissolution, and the requests are made to Divine Director and the Karmic Board.

The following process is shorter than usual and very powerful; few words are needed. Use it for any karma or karmic situations that still remain in your life or that of your Goddess or God. It may also be used for the ending of all karma with a particular person or entity who has done you or your Goddess or God harm. These are karmic releases for your core soul, and for you and your Goddess's or God's total Be-ing. When you are granted these releases, you may be shown the full origin of the situation at the time of your request or later. Request the Dissolution again when you know the whole story. Most of these Dissolutions and remaining karma involve Cosmic level or beyond core soul damage and its sources.

As with all other work involving karma, make your requests for one situation at a time and word them as simply as possible. The following requests are basic and for everyone, but be sure to also request Karmic Dissolution for every remaining suffering in your own life. Do the Universal Healings, as well. If a request is refused, try changing the wording, and also ask Divine Director for further information.

1. Ask to speak with Divine Director and the Karmic Board.

2. Request COSMIC AND BEYOND KARMIC DISSOLUTION FROM ALL CORE SOUL DAMAGE and its sources and perpetrators for you, your Goddess or God, your union, total union, and your ascension.

3. Ask for complete and total HEALING, REGENERATION AND KARMIC RENEWAL for all damage and destruction from the situation.

4. When the request has been granted, ASK TO EXTEND IT TO THE ALL—all Be-ings, all life, and all the Light—as needed. If you receive a "no" here, the request is not appropriate or not needed.

Universal Healing

a) When you feel that you have released all the remaining karma you are aware of, make the following request. Ask for COSMIC AND BEYOND COSMIC KARMIC DISSOLUTION FROM ALL REMAINING KARMA OF ALL KINDS AND ITS SOURCES AND PERPETRATORS—from the Earth and all planets, all Solar Systems, Galaxies, Universes and Cosmoses—for you, your Goddess or God, your union, total union and ascension. Request complete and total PURIFICATION, HEALING, REGENERATION AND KARMIC RENEWAL from all damage. If the request is denied, continue asking for Cosmic and Beyond Cosmic Karmic Dissolution from whatever issues arise—you will be given the information of what still needs to be cleared—and make the request again at another time.

b) Ask for complete COSMIC AND BEYOND COSMIC KARMIC DISSOLUTION FOR ALL OF THE LIGHT, AS APPROPRIATE AND NEEDED, from all remaining karma and its sources and perpetrators.

c) Ask for complete COSMIC AND BEYOND COSMIC KARMIC DISSOLUTION FROM ALL CHAINS OF EVIL and their members, and from all their spells, sorceries, negative and evil interference, all negative and evil use of energy of all types, all harm and damage of all types, and all replication of evil and harm in your energy through all lifetimes and between them. Make these requests for you, your Goddess or God, your union, total union and ascension. Request complete and total PURIFICATION, HEALING, REGENERATION AND COSMIC AND BEYOND COSMIC KARMIC RENEWAL for all that you have lost because of evil and the actions of evil, for you, your Goddess or God, your union, total union, and ascension.

d) Ask for complete COSMIC AND BEYOND COSMIC KARMIC DISSOLUTION FROM ALL MEMBERS AND ACTS OF ALL CHAINS OF EVIL FOR ALL OF THE ALL, AS APPROPRIATE AND NEEDED.

Process XIII   Cosmic Sword, Shield, Chalice Fusion

IN PROCESS II, YOUR DIMENSIONAL ARCHANGEL GIFTED YOU WITH THE SWORDS, Shields and Chalices of protection for the Dimensions of the Earth, Moon and Solar System for you, your Goddess or God, your union, total union, and ascension, and for your Galactic Cord and Grounding Cord systems. Your Interdimensional Archangel increased those protections with the Swords, Shields and Chalices of protection and healing through the Interdimensions of the Galaxy. When those protections were fused in Process III, they were automatically fused (the eighth Shield) with the protections of Archangel Metatron for full protection through the Universe, as well.

The Swords, Shields and Chalices of protection and healing for the Cosmos in all of its dimensions and interdimensions are to be requested from the Cosmic Archangels (Elohim) known as Purity and Astrea. These protections will be fused automatically (the eighth Shield again) by The Shekinah, the Great Cosmic Mother and Creator Goddess of our Cosmos. These protections provide additional and much needed safety for us, our Goddesses and Gods, our unions, total unions and ascensions, and our Galactic Cord and Grounding Cord systems, as well.

1. Ask to speak with Divine Director, the Karmic Board, and the Elohim Astrea and Purity. Request the REPROGRAMMING OF YOUR CREATION TO INSTALL YOUR COSMIC ELOHIM'S SWORD OF PROTECTION AND TRUTH IN YOUR ENERGY, YOUR GODDESS'S OR GOD'S ENERGY, IN THE ENERGY OF YOUR UNION, YOUR TOTAL UNION, YOUR ASCENSION, AND IN ALL GALACTIC CORD AND GROUNDING CORD SYS-TEMS IN THEIR COMPLETELY SYNCHRONIZED AND COM-PLEMENTARY STATE. The Sword's use is to fight evil in the Cosmos and beyond through all dimensions and between them. If at this step or any other of the process, your request is denied, ask what you must do to have it and follow the directions that will be given to you. Otherwise, continue.

2. If the request is granted, ask where the Sword is to be installed in each. There will be seven Swords, one in you, one in your Goddess or God, one in your union, one in your total union, one in your ascension, and one each in your Galactic Cord and Grounding Cord systems. They will be in seven different places. If the request is granted, but you are not shown's locations, you may still continue.

3. Ask that the reprogramming be completed and the Swords be installed.

4. Now REQUEST THE REPROGRAMMING OF YOUR CREATION TO INSTALL YOUR COSMIC ELOHIM'S KARMIC SHIELD IN YOUR ENERGY, YOUR GODDESS'S OR GOD'S ENERGY, IN THE ENERGY OF YOUR UNION, IN YOUR TOTAL UNION AND ASCENSION, AND IN ALL GALACTIC CORD AND GROUNDING CORD SYSTEMS IN THEIR COMPLETELY SYN-CHRONIZED AND COMPLEMENTARY STATE. There is one fur-ther Shield, provided by The Shekinah—that of the fusion of your combined Universal and Cosmic protections—to make a total of eight levels. The Shield protects you from the return of old karma from the Universe and Cosmos.

5. If the request is granted, ask where the Shield is to be installed in each. There will be seven Shields, one in you, one in your Goddess or God, one in your union, one in your total union, one in your ascension, and one each in your Galactic Cord and Grounding Cord systems. If you see the eighth, it will be sur-rounding all the others at the end of this process. The seven Shields will be in seven different places. If the request is granted, but you are not shown locations, you may still continue.

6. Ask that the reprogramming be completed and the Shields be installed.

7. Next, REQUEST THE REPROGRAMMING OF YOUR CRE-ATION TO INSTALL YOUR COSMIC ELOHIM'S CHALICE OF

HEALING AND REGENERATION IN YOUR ENERGY, YOUR GODDESS'S OR GOD'S ENERGY, IN THE ENERGY OF YOUR UNION, IN YOUR TOTAL UNION AND ASCENSION, AND IN ALL GALACTIC CORD AND GROUNDING CORD SYSTEMS IN THEIR COMPLETELY SYNCHRONIZED AND COMPLEMEN-TARY STATE. The Chalice's use is for automatic self-healing and karmic renewal of all core soul damage.

8. If the request is granted, ask where the Chalice is to be installed in each. There will be seven Chalices, one in you, one in your Goddess or God, one in your union, one in your total union, one in your ascension, and one each in your Galactic Cord and Grounding Cord systems. They will be in seven different places. If the request is granted, but you are not shown locations, you may still continue.

9. Ask that the reprogramming be completed and the Chalices be installed.

10. Now ask for THE FULL REPROGRAMMING OF YOUR CRE-ATION FOR THE FULL, CONTINUOUS AND PERMANENT ACTIVATION OF THE SWORDS, SHIELDS AND CHALICES IN YOUR ENERGY, IN YOUR GODDESS'S OR GOD'S ENERGY, IN THE ENERGY OF YOUR UNION, TOTAL UNION, AND ASCENSION, AND IN ALL GALACTIC CORD AND GROUND-ING CORD SYSTEMS FOREVER. Wait for this to be done; unless you receive a "no" response, it's happening. Ask when to go on.

11. Request the FULL AND FOREVER ACTIVATION of your COS-MIC Swords, Shields and Chalices.

12. When all seven Swords, eight Shields and seven Chalices in you, your Goddess or God, your union, total union and ascension, and all Galactic Cord and Grounding Cord systems are fully activated, request the following. Ask Divine Director, the Karmic Board, and the Elohim Astrea and Purity for THE FULL REPROGRAMMING OF YOUR CREATION TO MERGE AND FUSE, AND TO TRANSFIGURE THE MERGING AND FUSION OF THE

SWORDS, SHIELDS AND CHALICES. The seven Swords will be fused together, the eight Shields will be fused together, and the seven Chalices will be fused together. Ask when the fusion and transfiguration are complete; wait for this before going on.

13. Ask Divine Director, the Karmic Board, and the Elohim Astrea and Purity for the FULL REPROGRAMMING OF YOUR CREATION TO FULLY ACTIVATE THE FUSION AND TRANSFIGURATION OF THE SWORDS, SHIELDS AND CHALICES, AND THEREBY FULLY ACTIVATE AND TRANSFIGURE THE UNIVERSAL AND COSMIC PROTECTION OF YOUR UNION WITH YOUR GODDESS OR GOD. Wait for this to complete.

14. Now ask Divine Director, the Karmic Board, and the Elohim Astrea and Purity for the FULL REPROGRAMMING OF YOUR CREATION TO MERGE AND FUSE, AND TO TRANSFIGURE THE MERGING AND FUSION OF YOUR COSMIC AND UNIVERSAL SWORDS, SHIELDS AND CHALICES WITH THOSE OF YOUR DIMENSIONAL AND INTERDIMENSIONAL ARCHANGELS AND THE ARCHANGEL METATRON. Wait for this to be done; unless you receive a "no" response, it's happening. Ask when to go on.

15. Ask Divine Director, the Karmic Board, and the Elohim Astrea and Purity for the FULL REPROGRAMMING OF YOUR CREATION TO FULLY ACTIVATE THE FUSION AND TRANSFIGURATION OF THE COMBINED SWORDS, SHIELDS AND CHALICES AS ABOVE, AND THEREBY FULLY ACTIVATE AND TRANSFIGURE YOUR UNION WITH YOUR GODDESS OR GOD. Request also to FULLY ACTIVATE AND TRANSFIGURE THE TOTAL PROTECTION OF YOU, YOUR GODDESS OR GOD, YOUR UNION, TOTAL UNION AND ASCENSION, AND ALL GALACTIC CORD AND GROUNDING CORD SYSTEMS IN THEIR COMPLETELY SYNCHRONIZED AND COMPLEMENTARY STATE FOREVER. Wait for this to complete.

16. Request these healings and reprogrammings in the name of the Light, immediately and instantly, past, present and future, forever and NOW. (No other finishing process is required.)

17. Thank Divine Director, the Karmic Board, the Elohim Astrea and Purity, your Dimensional and Interdimensional Archangels, Archangel Metatron, and our Great Cosmic Mother The Shekinah.

Universal Healings

a) Repeat the full process above, but instead of doing it for *your* creation and energy, do it for ALL CREATION AND ALL ENERGY OF THE LIGHT, AS APPROPRIATE AND NEEDED.

b) Do the full process above, wording it for THE CREATION OF ALL THE GODDESSES AND GODS, AS APPROPRI- ATE AND NEEDED.

c) Do the full process above, wording it for THE CREATION OF ALL THE GODDESS/GOD UNIONS, GREAT GOD- DESS/GOD UNIONS, AND FOR ALL BE-INGS OF THE LIGHT, AS APPROPRIATE AND NEEDED.

d) Repeat the process again, wording it for THE CREATION AND ENERGY OF THE EARTH, MOON, SOLAR SYSTEM, GALAXY, UNIVERSE, THE COSMOS AND BEYOND, AND FOR ALL LIFE, ALL BE-INGS, AND ALL THE LIGHT, AS APPROPRIATE AND NEEDED FOR EACH.

e) Repeat the process once more, requesting the REPRO- GRAMMING OF YOUR CREATION TO INSTALL YOUR UNIVERSAL AND COSMIC SWORDS, SHIELDS AND CHALICES IN YOUR HOME, GARDEN, CAR, COM- PUTER, BELONGINGS, PETS AND CHILDREN. (Adults living in the home must make the requests for themselves.) Make sure the articles of protection are all installed and are fully and forever activated.

Process XIV Cancelling Outdated Vows

WE ALL MAKE VOWS—SWORN PROMISES TO ALWAYS OR NEVER DO A PARTICULAR thing. Some vows seem to be only "expressions of speech" at the time, while others are made at moments of high emotion, pain or stress. With these types of vows, we may not even be aware that we have made them or of the consequences of having done so. Some vows are religious. Many vows that are appropriate at the time they are made become inappropriate later, in other lifetimes or other situations. Some vows that we make without forethought are inappropriate from the time they are created. Some vows are no longer positive because their purpose has been finished.

All vows are karmic. Once created they become a part of your Akashic Record and they and their consequences perpetuate from lifetime to lifetime. It requires a conscious request to reverse and uncreate a vow. Since vows made in other lifetimes or made inadvertently may not be evident, it is important to discover and reverse all vows no longer positive for you to continue to keep.

Outdated vows can hold back your ascension or any other aspect of your life and personal growth. A vow of poverty made in a monastic or convent situation is positive in that situation, but can wreak havoc at another time when you need to make an unsupported living. Reacting to a difficult relationship with a vow to always be alone may leave you too alone in another lifetime when you wish for a mate. If you are in a Goddess or God Union, both your vows and those of your Goddess or God need to be examined. The process below describes how to uncreate a vow no longer good for you to keep.

If you are, or have ever been, a Buddhist or interested in Buddhist teachings you may have taken the Bodhisattva Vow. On the surface this vow seems quite positive, as it states that you will work for the enlightenment of all Be-ings and defer your own enlightenment until everyone is freed from the requirement to reincarnate. Enlightenment is ascension, however. This vow may prevent the completion of your ascension process, and the completion of your Goddess or God Union. When Brede showed me the consequences of the Bodhisattva Vow in myself, She also showed me that She Herself had made an additional Buddhist vow—to take on the suffering of all Be-ings. Not only was the completion of our union obstructed by my Bodhisattva Vow, but Brede's vow explained both Her and my great suffering in this and other lifetimes.

Both vows were made in another time, when ascension or enlightenment was not completed in the body during incarnation, as it is now, but resulted in death with no return to help others. It is of far more benefit to complete your ascension and remain alive and in body with your Goddess or God beside you to teach and heal than it would be to delay your individual ascension until everyone else is ready. With the understanding that these and many other vows are outdated and no longer positive in our current New Age, it is important to discover and release them.

1. Ask to speak with Divine Director and the Karmic Board.

2. Request the REPROGRAMMING OF YOUR COSMIC AND BEYOND COSMIC CREATION FOR THE KARMIC DISSOLUTION OF ALL VOWS HOLDING BACK OR PREVENTING THE COMPLETION OF YOUR ASCENSION AND YOUR UNION WITH YOUR GODDESS OR GOD. Make the request for you, your Goddess or God, your union, total union and your ascension. When you receive a "yes," go on.

3. Request the REPROGRAMMING OF YOUR COSMIC AND BEYOND COSMIC CREATION FOR THE KARMIC DISSOLUTION OF ALL VOWS KNOWN AND UNKNOWN THAT ARE NO LONGER POSITIVE for you, your Goddess or God, your union, total union, and ascension.

4. Request the REPROGRAMMING OF YOUR COSMIC AND BEYOND COSMIC CREATION FOR THE KARMIC DISSOLUTION OF THE BODHISATTVA VOW IF YOU HAVE MADE IT IN THIS OR ANY OTHER LIFETIME. Request Karmic

Dissolution also for any vows to take on the suffering of others or of the All. These requests are for you, your Goddess or God, your union, total union, and your ascension.

5. If you are aware of any other specific vows you may have made, request the REPROGRAMMING OF YOUR COSMIC AND BEYOND COSMIC CREATION FOR THE KARMIC DISSOLU-TION OF EACH OF THESE VOWS. Ask your Goddess or God what vows She or He has made that need to be released, and make the request for Her or Him as above. All requests are for you, your Goddess or God, your union, total union, and your ascension. When the vow was made by your Goddess or God, make the request for Her or Him first, then for you, your Goddess or God, your union, total union, and ascension.

6. Ask if there are any of your vows remaining that have not been released by the requests above, and that still need to be released. If there are, ask for the information you need to gain Cosmic and Beyond Cosmic Karmic Dissolution from them, and make the requests. If there are not, ask if there are any vows remaining for your Goddess or God that have not been released by the requests above, and that still need to be released. If there are, ask for the information you need to gain Cosmic and Beyond Cosmic Karmic Dissolution from them and make the requests. Do this individu-ally also for your union, total union, and your ascension. When all outdated vows are cancelled, go on.

7. Now request of all the vows above, that they be UNCREATED AND REVERSED BY THE LIGHT ALONG WITH ALL THEIR NEGATIVE AND EVIL EFFECTS.

8. Request THE HEALING OF ALL DAMAGE FROM ALL VOWS for you, your Goddess or God, your union, total union and ascen-sion. Request COMPLETE KARMIC RENEWAL AND RESTORA-TION OF YOUR COSMIC AND BEYOND COSMIC CREATIONAL BIRTHRIGHT OF ABSOLUTE PURITY for you,

your Goddess or God, your union, total union, and ascension.

9. Request the COMPLETION OF YOUR ASCENSION AND YOUR GODDESS/GOD UNION, AND THE FULL INCARNATION AND MANIFESTATION OF YOUR GODDESS OR GOD WITH AND THROUGH YOU NOW AND FOREVER. Request COSMIC AND BEYOND COSMIC KARMIC DISSOLUTION FROM ANYTHING AND EVERYTHING THAT MAY BE HOLDING BACK OR PRE-VENTING THE ABOVE.

10. Thank Divine Director and the Karmic Board.

Universal Healings

a) Use the process above for the Cosmic and Beyond Cosmic Karmic Dissolution of ALL VOWS OF POVERTY.

b) Repeat the process above for the Cosmic and Beyond Cosmic Karmic Dissolution of ALL VOWS OF BEING ALONE.

c) Repeat the process above for the Cosmic and Beyond Cosmic Karmic Dissolution of ALL VOWS OF REVENGE OR RETRIBUTION.

d) Ask for all of the above for ALL BE-INGS, ALL LIFE, ALL THE LIGHT, AND FOR ALL OF THE ALL, as appropriate and needed.

e) Repeat the process above for the Cosmic and Beyond Cosmic Karmic Dissolution of ALL VOWS MADE AGAINST YOU, your Goddess or God, your union, total union, and ascension by others. This is extremely important to request.

Process XV Cancelling Curses

LIKE VOWS, CURSES AND OTHER NEGATIVE OR EVIL USES OF ENERGY CAN BE insidious, and they can be made almost inadvertently in times of high emotion. Unlike vows, however, curses are much more often made against you than made by you, and they have happened frequently in our many lifetimes. I use the term "negative or evil uses of energy" to include all curses, spells, hexes, all rituals done with harmful intent, all uses of symbols to do harm, all psychic attacks, and all other forms of negative and evil interference of every kind and type.

We have dealt with all of these issues in other processes, particularly in *Essential Energy Balancing II* and *Reliance on the Light*. The difference here is in taking the releases and Karmic Dissolutions through your Creational Programming at the level of the Cosmic and Beyond Cosmic Creational energy of your soul. The two processes that follow are meant to complete the release of all negative and evil interference, both given and received, from your creational energy. Most of this interference has been done to you, rather than done by you.

1. Ask to speak with Divine Director and the Karmic Board.

2. Request the REPROGRAMMING OF YOUR COSMIC AND BEYOND COSMIC CREATION FOR THE KARMIC DISSOLUTION OF ALL CURSES, SPELLS, HEXES, NEGATIVE AND EVIL USE OF RITUAL, NEGATIVE AND EVIL USE OF SYMBOLS, PSYCHIC ATTACKS, AND ALL OTHER FORMS OF NEGATIVE AND EVIL INTERFERENCE AND ENERGY USE BOTH GIVEN AND RECEIVED for you, your Goddess and God, your union, total union and ascension. This is to include all instances, known and unknown, existing in all levels of your Akashic Record from the creation of your soul until the present. It includes all lifetimes and between them, and all states of existence, in the past, present, future, forever and now. Wait for the "yes" with each step before going on.

3. If you need to know about specific instances of the above misuse of energy, either done to you or done by you, STATE THAT YOU ARE WILLING TO HAVE THE AWARENESS and that you request total Cosmic and Beyond Cosmic Karmic Dissolution and release from all instances. This information may come now or later.

4. Request that all the negatives and evils above, both given and received, be UNCREATED AND REVERSED BY THE LIGHT ALONG WITH ALL OF THEIR NEGATIVE AND EVIL EFFECTS, for you, your Goddess or God, your union, total union, and ascension.

5. Request TOTAL HEALING OF ALL DAMAGE FROM ALL THE NEG-ATIVES AND EVILS ABOVE. Also request complete KARMIC RENEWAL AND RESTORATION OF YOUR COSMIC AND BEYOND COSMIC CREATIONAL BIRTHRIGHT OF ABSOLUTE PURITY, for you, your Goddess or God, your union, total union, and ascension.

6. Ask for the COMPLETION OF YOUR ASCENSION AND YOUR GODDESS OR GOD UNION, AND THE FULL INCARNATION AND MANIFESTATION OF YOUR GODDESS OR GOD WITH AND THROUGH YOU, NOW AND FOREVER. Ask for COSMIC AND BEYOND COSMIC KARMIC DISSOLUTION FROM ANY-THING AND EVERYTHING THAT MAY BE HOLDING BACK OR PREVENTING THESE COMPLETIONS, for you, your Goddess or God, your union, total union, and ascension.

7. Thank Divine Director and the Karmic Board.

Universal Healings

a) Request the above process for ALL BE-INGS, ALL LIFE, ALL THE LIGHT, AND FOR ALL OF THE ALL, as appropriate and needed.

b) Request that ALL CURSES AND NEGATIVE AND EVIL USE OF ENERGY IN ALL INSTANCES BE MADE CREATION-ALLY VOID and having no effect on any. Ask for this for ALL BE-INGS, ALL LIFE, ALL THE LIGHT, AND FOR ALL OF THE ALL, as appropriate and needed.

Process XVI Final Clearing

BY NOW, SUCH THINGS AS NEGATIVE AND EVIL ENTITIES AND ATTACHMENTS SHOULD be a thing of the past—but are they? This final clearing is to make sure that all such negative and evil discarnates are fully gone, and that none will ever return. It is also a protection from new negative or evil energies entering your aura or your home. This is a final cleansing that goes all the way back to the "other Cosmos" where we and our Goddesses and Gods originated. The process is a clearing and protection for the Goddesses and Gods as much as it is for us.

With Process IX in *Essential Energy Balancing I,* all discarnate evil and interference that originated from Earth and Solar System karma was cleared from your energy. With the process that follows, all remaining discarnate interference will be cleared from your karma and your energy from all planets, galaxies, the Universe, Cosmos and beyond. You may be aware of negative or evil energies leaving with this process. They will now be destroyed and ended forever.

1. Ask to speak with Divine Director and the Karmic Board.

2. Request for you, your Goddess or God, your union, total union and ascension the REPROGRAMMING OF YOUR COSMIC AND BEYOND COSMIC CREATION FOR KARMIC DISSOLUTION FROM:

    all attachments
    all negative and evil entities or discarnates
    all possessions and possessing entities
    all negative and evil elementals
    all negative and evil alien influence and implants
    all negative and evil past life or between life artifacts
    all negative and evil energy of all types
    all negative and evil interference of all types

The request is to include all negative and evil effects from the list above. It also includes everything negative and evil that has come to you from other people, places or Be-ings in any way, or while doing healing for any Be-ings, for the Earth, Moon, Solar System, Galaxy, Universe, Cosmos and beyond.

These dissolutions are also to include and protect your home, garden, car, computer, belongings, pets and children—and every aspect of your life.

3. Ask to ANNIHILATE, EXTINGUISH, UNCREATE AND OBLITERATE all of the above negative and evil energies and entities immediately and forever. If any of these are not to be destroyed, they are to be removed from your energy forever and passed over (or under) for dealing with as the Light deems appropriate.

4. Request that ALL NEGATIVITY AND EVIL AND THEIR EFFECTS BE UNCREATED AND REVERSED BY THE LIGHT and that your energy be FULLY PURIFIED.

5. Ask for the TOTAL HEALING OF ALL DAMAGE AND DESTRUCTION FROM ALL THE NEGATIVES AND EVILS ABOVE. Also request complete KARMIC RENEWAL FOR YOUR COSMIC AND BEYOND COSMIC CREATIONAL BIRTHRIGHT OF ABSOLUTE PURITY AND PERFECTION IN THE LIGHT.

6. Ask for the COMPLETION AND OPENING OF YOUR ASCENSION AND YOUR GODDESS OR GOD UNION, AND FOR THE FULL INCARNATION AND MANIFESTATION OF YOUR GODDESS OR GOD WITH AND THROUGH YOU, NOW AND FOREVER. Ask for COSMIC AND BEYOND COSMIC KARMIC DISSOLUTION FROM ANYTHING AND EVERYTHING THAT MAY BE HOLDING BACK OR PREVENTING THESE COMPLETIONS, for you, your Goddess or God, your union, total union, and ascension.

7. Thank Divine Director and the Karmic Board.

Universal Healings

a) Request the above process for ALL BE-INGS, ALL LIFE, ALL THE LIGHT, AND FOR ALL OF THE ALL, as appropriate and needed.

Process XVII Planetary Re-Creation and Activation

IN THE MULTI-COSMIC AND BEYOND WAR BETWEEN THE CHAINS OF LIGHT AND Chains of Evil, the Master Plans (Light Beyond) and blueprints for Goddess and God manifestation on the Earth were destroyed by evil. With it was destroyed not only all Be-ings' connections to Goddess, God and the Light, but the means to recreate those connections. The process that follows is the request to recreate the blueprints and the means for restoring the Goddess/God Unions.

1. Ask to speak with Divine Director, the Karmic Board, Nada, Earth Mother, Light Mother, and St. Germaine.

2. Ask for COSMIC AND BEYOND COSMIC CREATIONAL REPATTERNING FOR ALL THE LIGHT TO RECREATE IN ABSOLUTE PURITY AND PERFECTION ALL BLUEPRINTS AND MASTER PLANS FOR THE GREAT GODDESS'S RETURN TO MANIFEST AND INCARNATE FULLY ON EARTH.

3. Also request COSMIC AND BEYOND COSMIC CREATIONAL REPATTERNING FOR ALL THE LIGHT TO RECREATE IN ABSOLUTE PURITY AND PERFECTION ALL BLUEPRINTS AND MASTER PLANS FOR ALL GODDESSES' AND GODS' RETURN TO MANIFEST AND INCARNATE FULLY ON EARTH with and through their chosen people and on their own in absolute safety and Light.

4. Request COSMIC AND BEYOND COSMIC CREATIONAL REPATTERNING TO RECREATE IN ABSOLUTE PURITY AND PERFECTION OF THE LIGHT ALL REQUIRED CONNECTIONS, CORDS, COMPONENTS AND SYSTEMS for the Earth and all Earth Be-ings to accomplish the above.

5. Next, ask for COSMIC AND BEYOND COSMIC CREATIONAL REPATTERNING IN ABSOLUTE PURITY AND PERFECTION OF THE LIGHT FOR THE EARTH, ALL BE-INGS AND ALL LIFE

TO FULLY AND TOTALLY PROTECT THE NEW CREATIONAL BLUEPRINTS AND ALL THEIR CONNECTIONS, CORDS, COMPONENTS AND SYSTEMS in the Earth, all Be-ings and all life. Also ask for the total protection of all those bringing in the Goddesses and Gods, all the Goddesses and Gods, all the Goddess/God Unions, total unions, and ascensions.

6. Ask for COSMIC AND BEYOND COSMIC KARMIC RENEWAL AND TOTAL RESTORATION FOR THE RETURN OF THE GREAT GODDESS, ALL THE GODDESSES AND GODS, AND ALL THE LIGHT TO THE EARTH, MOON, SOLAR SYSTEM, GALAXY, UNIVERSE, COSMOS AND BEYOND IN ABSOLUTE PURITY, PERFECTION AND SAFETY FOR THE LIGHT FOR-EVER.

7. Request the full ESTABLISHMENT, CONNECTION, ACTIVA-TION AND OPENING of all of the above, immediately and instantly, past, present and future, forever and NOW.

8. Request the full ESTABLISHMENT, CONNECTION, ACTIVA-TION AND OPENING of all who are bringing in the Goddesses and Gods, of all the Goddesses and Gods, of all the Goddess and God Unions, total unions and ascensions, and of all Great Goddess/God Unions immediately and instantly, past, present and future, forever and NOW.

9. Ask that the Earth and all of the above be TRANSFIGURED AGAINST ALL EVIL FOREVER, FOR THE LIGHT FOREVER, AND UNTO THE LIGHT AND UNTO PROTECTION FOREVER.

10. Request COSMIC AND BEYOND COSMIC KARMIC DISSOLU-TION FROM ANYTHING AND EVERYTHING THAT MAY BE HOLDING BACK, DELAYING, OBSTRUCTING OR PREVENT-ING THESE HEALINGS for all of the above and for the Earth.

11. Ask for these things in the name of the Light for you, your Goddess or God, your union, total union and ascension, for the

Earth, all Be-ings, all life, and for the All, immediately and instantly, past, present and future, forever and NOW.

12. Thank Divine Director, the Karmic Board, Nada, Earth Mother, Light Mother and St. Germaine.

Universal Healings

a) Request COSMIC AND BEYOND COSMIC KARMIC DISSOLUTION FROM BEING SEPARATED FROM YOUR GODDESS OR GOD AND FROM THE CHAIN OF LIGHT, for you, your Goddess or God, your union, total union, and ascension.

Process XVIII   Resurrection

WE ARE THE CREATIONS OF OUR GODDESSES, WHO IN TURN WERE CREATED BY Goddesses at even higher levels than theirs. For this Cosmos, this lineage of Light originates with our Great Cosmic Mother, The Shekinah, and the four Differentiated Goddesses of the Below (Aleyah, Persephone, Nepthys, Aiyisha). Beyond this Cosmos it extends to many other Creator Goddesses and Gods. Because of Evil Duality, the soul mutations that generated evil duplication of every creation of the Light, our Goddesses incarnated us at a reduced Light level, a level too low to cause activation of Evil Twins. This was done for our survival and protection, and for the protection of our Goddesses and all of the Light. We were therefore also created at too low a Light vibration for complete ascension or to bring our Goddesses or Gods into us deeply enough to fully incarnate them in our bodies.

Now that Evil Duality has been destroyed and ended in all souls and soul lineages, our Light can be raised to the level needed to bring in our Goddesses and Gods, and to restore our true Creational Birthrights and our ascensions. The process is called Resurrection—it is the resurrection of our own souls in our bodies. This raising of our Light is the last step before the completion and opening of our Goddess and God Unions. With the Light of our souls "turned on," we become in truth the Goddesses and Gods that we were meant to be. The process that follows takes about eight hours for completion, and the opening of your Goddess or God Union follows it. You will feel it happening. Resurrection will not be initiated until all other preparatory work has been finished.

This request is best made at night in bed, the last thing before sleep. It may be preceded by a full Essential Energy Balancing Daily Process (see Appendix II). If you become aware of entities or Be-ings, even animal hybrids, in or around your energies, and are told that they are not of the Light—ask that they be destroyed and obliterated in totality.

1. Ask to speak with Divine Director and the Karmic Board, Nada, Light Mother, The Shekinah, and your Goddess or God. It is permitted at this time to directly speak with The Shekinah; do so only with the greatest respect.

2. Request the RESURRECTION OF YOUR FULLY HEALED SOUL in your body and the turning on of your Light.

3. Request that YOUR SOUL BE RESURRECTED IN A TOTALLY PURE AND PERFECT STATE, without evil or negative mutations of any kind, and without damage, destruction, or negative or evil effects.

4. Request that YOUR SOUL BE RESURRECTED IN YOUR BODY TOTALLY CLEANSED OF ALL EVIL AND NEGATIVITY, AND OF ALL ACTIVATION OF EVIL, NEGATIVITY, DAMAGE OR DESTRUCTION, from all sources and from the original source of evil mutation (the Source of all Evil and all its creations and manifestations).

5. Ask that your soul be CLEARED AND HEALED OF ALL REMAINING IMPRINTS OF THE DAMAGE AND SUFFERING CAUSED BY NEGATIVITY, EVIL AND EVIL DUALITY through all your lifetimes and between them. These imprints may include (but are not limited to) such patterns as fear, terror, grief, pain, rage, trauma, past abuse, and helplessness. They are to be removed and dissolved in totality now and all remaining damage and destruction to your soul fully healed.

6. Request the FULL RECONNECTION, ABSOLUTE AND TOTAL PROTECTION, FULL MANIFESTATION, AND COMPLETE ACTIVATION OF YOUR SOUL AND SOUL MATRIX, AND THEIR FULL MANIFESTATION IN YOUR BODY. Ask for all that is needed of healing, regeneration, re-creation and replacement of components, connections, blueprints, processes and functions of and through all systems. Request full activation and the full restoration of your soul's Light and of your own. Ask that the

Light be turned on, and request the full opening of your connections with your soul.

7. Ask to know YOUR TRUE NAME, your soul's name. It is not your name for this incarnation, and it is not the name of your Goddess or God. You are a part of your Goddess (male or female) and were created by Her, but you are not Her. You may be surprised to know who you really are.

8. Request the COMPLETION AND FOREVER OPENING OF YOUR ENERGY, YOUR GODDESS'S OR GOD'S ENERGY, AND THAT OF YOUR UNION, TOTAL UNION AND ASCENSION. Request the full incarnation of your Goddess or God into and through you to live with you on Earth. (This is different from your soul's resurrection, but especially in the case of a God, resurrection must precede it.)

9. Ask for these things in the name of the Light and in the absolute purity and perfection of the Light, under Karmic Law, and through all the ripples of Be-ing and time, past, present and future, forever and NOW.

10. Thank Divine Director, the Karmic Board, Nada, Light Mother, The Shekinah, and your Goddess or God. Also thank the protectors and guides of your total union. Your energy—and that of your Goddess or God, your union, total union and ascension—will now be activated, merged, fused, fully protected, and transfigured unto the Light forever.

Universal Healings

a) Request the process above for ALL SOULS, AND FOR THE CREATION AND MATRIX OF ALL SOULS.

b) Make the requests above for THE EARTH AND ALL PLANETS, our Moon and all Moons, our Solar System and all Solar Systems, our Galaxy and all Galaxies, our Universe and all Universes, our Cosmos and all Cosmoses, and beyond and between.

c) Make the requests above for THE IS AND THE IS-NOT, THE VOID AND THE NONVOID, for all Light, sound, frequencies, vibrations, energies, and creations, and everything in between.

d) Make the requests above for ALL ASPECTS OF SPACE AND BETWEEN THEM, including Deep Space, Hyperspace, the Void of Space, and the spaces between molecules and atoms.

e) Make the requests above for all Be-ings, all life and all the Light, as appropriate and needed for each, THROUGH ALL THE RIPPLES OF BE-ING AND TIME, AND BETWEEN THEM.

Process XIX   Soul Healing

THE HEALINGS OF THE ESSENTIAL ENERGY BALANCING SYSTEM TO THIS POINT
have worked through the layers and levels of the soul. All that remains to
clear and heal is the Matrix of the soul itself, and the following process is
the method for doing so. Resurrecting your soul into your body (Process
XVIII) awakens what is still needed of soul healing.

The Soul Matrix is the structure of the soul, consisting of the Crystal
Shaft outer sheath and the Tube of Light which contains all the other
anatomy and levels. These include all the layers and bodies, chakra systems,
template systems and portals, processes, circuitry and the connections
among them. Every part of you, your Goddess or God, your union, total
union, and your ascension are within the Crystal Shaft and Tube of Light, as
well as all other members of your soul group or Soul Family including your
pets. A soul group contains many people and many Goddesses and Gods.
The Soul Matrix also consists of all connections to your Chain of Light and
to every Light Be-ing, as well as all of your connections to the Earth, and
from Earth through the Cosmos and beyond. If you could see your soul
from the outside, it would appear as a tall obelisk of gleaming light, irides-
cent white with every possible color moving through it.

Soul healing must encompass the many realities—including simultaneous, alternate and blister realities—of the many lifetimes experienced
by each and every soul group member, and between them. The healing
process that follows will effect healing in every member of your soul
group, known and unknown.

The following process is the beginning prototype for all soul healing
requests. Use it from here on for all requests of every type that you may
have and for all the unhealed issues remaining in your life.

1. Ask to speak with Divine Director and the Karmic Board. (They
   will be your liaison to The Shekinah and to the Creator Goddesses
   beyond. Do not approach The Shekinah or other Creator
   Goddesses directly, but only through them.)

2. Ask for DIVINE DISSOLUTION from all that obstructs, delays, withholds, or blocks the full potential of your soul.

3. Request to UNMAKE ALL BLUEPRINTS AND ENCODINGS THAT ARE NOT OF THE ABSOLUTE PERFECTION OF THE LIGHT.

4. Request CLEANSING, CLEARING AND PURIFICATION TO THE TOTALITY OF THE LIGHT.

5. Ask for ALL THAT IS NEEDED OF HEALING AND REGENERATION, REPLACEMENT, RE-CREATION, CONNECTION AND RECONNECTION, ACTIVATION, RESURRECTION, UNION, ONENESS AND OPENING; NEW ENCODINGS, BLUEPRINTS, DOWNLOADINGS, PROCESSES, COMPONENTS, PROTECTIONS, PROGRAMMINGS AND SYSTEMS; AND ALL ELSE THAT MAY BE NEEDED, named and unnamed, known and unknown, in the perfection and glory of the Light.

6. Ask for DIVINE RENEWAL AND RESTORATION, DIVINE GRACE AND ABSOLUTION, AS NEEDED.

7. Request these healings FOR YOU, YOUR GODDESS OR GOD, YOUR UNION, TOTAL UNION, AND ASCENSION, FOR ALL RESURRECTIONS OF THE LIGHT, ALL MEMBERS OF YOUR SOUL GROUP, FOR YOUR SOUL, and for all your connections with the Light, with the Earth, and with all that's Light within all Cosmoses.

8. Request these healings THROUGH ALL CONCENTRIC CIRCLES OF REALITIES, INCLUDING BLISTER REALITIES, SIMULTANEOUS REALITIES, MULTIPLE REALITIES, ALL STATES OF EXISTENCE AND BETWEEN THEM, AND ALL OVERLAPS, INTERFACES, CONNECTIONS, AND BETWEEN THEM.

9. Ask for these healings through the PAST, PRESENT AND FUTURE, FOREVER AND NOW, IMMEDIATELY AND INSTANTLY, THROUGH ALL INFINITY AND ETERNITY, AND EVERYTHING IN BETWEEN.

10. Thank Divine Director, the Karmic Board and The Shekinah.

Universal Healings

a) Make the request above for ALL SOULS AND ALL MEM-
BERS OF ALL SOUL GROUPS OF THE LIGHT.

b) Use the process above to make the same request for the
SOUL OF THE EARTH HERSELF, and all other structures
including our Moon and all Moons, our Solar System and
all Solar Systems, our Galaxy and all Galaxies, our Universe
and all Universes, our Cosmos and all Cosmoses, and all
Multi-Cosmoses and beyond.

c) Repeat the process again for ALL OF THE ALL OF THE
LIGHT, as appropriate and needed for each.

d) Use this process to heal ALL THE ILLS OF THE PLANET,
one at a time, every wrong that you can think of.

e) Use this process to heal ALL OF YOUR OWN ILLS, PHYS-
ICAL AND OTHERWISE, one at a time, everything that
you need, everything that still remains.

f) Use this process for DIVINE DISSOLUTION FROM PEO-
PLE AND BE-INGS WHO HAVE CAUSED YOU GREAT
HARM. Ask permission first for each: Karmic Dissolution
may be enough.

Process XX Multi-Cosmic Expansion

THE FOLLOWING PROCESS IS TO EXPAND ALL PREVIOUS REQUESTS FROM *ESSENTIAL Energy Balancing I, II* and *III* to include all the levels of Be-ing and raise all requests (as appropriate and needed) through Multi-Cosmic and beyond Multi-Cosmic Creational levels. The structural creational levels include: Earth and all planets, our Moon and all Moons, our Solar System and all Solar Systems, our Galaxy and all Galaxies, our Cosmos and all Cosmos's, our and all Multi-Cosmoses, and our and all Multi-Cosmic Systems and beyond. This process is a Creational Repatterning and Reprogramming of the entire soul system and of all your soul's connections with all of the Light, Above and Below.

Because of the Reprogramming, and the requests for Transfiguration Against All Evil forever, for the Light forever, and unto the Light and unto Protection forever, you may experience the closing of your crown chakra for about three days. Nevertheless, this process is particularly important to do as it extends your protections and all other healings to the highest possible levels and completes your clearing from evil.

1. Ask to speak with Divine Director. Many other Be-ings of the Light will be involved, but Divine Director is our liaison to all of the Above.

2. Request to REPLACE AND RE-CREATE THE PROGRAMMING OF YOUR MULTI-COSMIC CREATION, AND CREATION ON ALL LEVELS AND THROUGH ALL STRUCTURES AND SYSTEMS, ALL YOUR ENERGY AND ALL YOUR SOUL, TO EXPAND ALL PREVIOUS REQUESTS AS APPROPRIATE THROUGH ALL MULTI-COSMIC LEVELS AND BEYOND. Ask for these things for you, your Goddess or God, your union, total union, ascension, resurrection, every member of your soul group, and your entire soul system.

These requests are all-encompassing as needed, and include but are not limited to: all Swords, Chalices and Shields, all protections of all kinds on all levels and for all systems and between them. They include all removal and destruction of all evil Be-ings and acts, all evil perpetuality, and the Source of All Evil and its creations, manifestations, effects and results on every level and between levels. The requests also include making the Essential Energy Balancing Daily Process (*Essential Energy Balancing, Process II*) a perpetual and permanent healing, and extending all Essential Healing Circles (*Essential Energy Balancing,* Process V) to all levels, as needed.

3. Ask to TRANSFIGURE YOUR NEW MULTI-COSMIC AND BEYOND MULTI-COSMIC CREATION AND TOTAL HEALING, YOUR SOUL, AND ALL OF YOUR ENERGY AND SOUL SYSTEMS ON ALL LEVELS AND BETWEEN LEVELS, AGAINST THE SOURCE OF ALL EVIL AND ALL ITS CREATIONS AND MANIFESTATIONS FOREVER, FOR THE LIGHT FOREVER, AND UNTO THE LIGHT AND UNTO PROTECTION FOREVER.

4. Request to TIGHTEN THE LIFE WEBS OF YOUR BE-ING AND SOUL in every aspect and through every level and system to make them invulnerable forever to all penetration, permeation, interference, damage or destruction, alteration or mutation, negative or evil sealing or re-routing, taint or contamination, generation of Evil Duality and duplications, and every other purpose, process, intent, and effect of evil.

5. Ask for DIVINE DISSOLUTION from The Source of All Evil and all its creations and manifestations, from all evil, all Evil Duality, and from all purposes, processes, intents, effects and results of evil and negativity that still remain in your energy and soul system, from all perpetrators and all sources, origins, and combinations.

6. Request to DESTROY AND OBLITERATE ALL BLUEPRINTS AND ENCODINGS ON ALL LEVELS AND THROUGH ALL SYS-

TEMS THAT ARE NOT OF THE GLORY AND PERFECTION OF THE LIGHT.

7. Ask for CLEANSING, CLEARING AND PURIFICATION TO THE TOTALITY OF THE LIGHT.

8. Ask for ALL THAT IS NEEDED OF HEALING AND REGENERA-TION, REPLACEMENT, RE-CREATION, CONNECTION AND RECONNECTION, ACTIVATION, RESURRECTION, UNION AND OPENING; NEW ENCODINGS, BLUEPRINTS, DOWN-LOADINGS, PROCESSES, COMPONENTS, PROTECTIONS, PROGRAMMINGS, COMPUTERS AND SYSTEMS; AND ALL ELSE THAT MAY BE NEEDED, NAMED AND UNNAMED, KNOWN AND UNKNOWN, IN THE PERFECTION AND GLORY OF THE LIGHT.

9. Request DIVINE RENEWAL AND RESTORATION IN ALL THINGS, AND DIVINE GRACE AND ABSOLUTION AS NEEDED.

10. Request these healings for YOU, YOUR GODDESS OR GOD, YOUR UNION, TOTAL UNION, AND ASCENSION, ALL RES-URRECTIONS OF THE LIGHT, ALL MEMBERS OF YOUR SOUL GROUP, FOR YOUR SOUL, for all your connections with the Light, with the Earth, and with all that's Light within all Cosmoses.

11. Ask for these healings THROUGH ALL CONCENTRIC CIRCLES OF ALL REALITIES, INCLUDING BLISTER REALITIES, SIMUL-TANEOUS REALITIES, MULTIPLE REALITIES, ALL STATES OF EXISTENCE AND BETWEEN THEM, AND ALL OVERLAPS, INTERFACES, CONNECTIONS, AND BETWEEN THEM.

12. Ask for these healings through the PAST, PRESENT AND FUTURE, FOREVER AND NOW, IMMEDIATELY AND INSTANTLY, THROUGH ALL INFINITY AND ETERNITY, AND EVERYTHING IN BETWEEN.

13. Thank Divine Director and all Be-ings of the Light.

Universal Healings

a) Make the request above for ALL SOULS AND ALL MEMBERS OF ALL SOUL GROUPS OF THE LIGHT.

b) Use the process above to make the same request for ALL BE-INGS OF ALL REALMS OF THE LIGHT, INDIVIDUALLY AND COLLECTIVELY, ABOVE AND BELOW, and for all Be-ings, all Life and all the Light.

c) Make the request above for the SOUL OF THE EARTH AND OF ALL OTHER STRUCTURES, CREATIONS AND SYSTEMS, including our Moon and all Moons, our Solar System and all Solar Systems, our Galaxy and all Galaxies, our Universe and all Universes, our Cosmos and all Cosmoses, and all Multi-Cosmoses and beyond.

d) Repeat the request again for ALL OF THE ALL OF THE LIGHT, as appropriate and needed for each.

Process XXI Multi-Cosmic Activation

THIS PROCESS IS TO ACTIVATE YOUR SOUL, YOUR ENERGY SYSTEMS AND ALL components on all levels, your Goddess or God Union, total union, ascension, and resurrection. Its purpose is to open you to the Light in every way appropriate, to restore full and optimal function in complete purity, and to complete the incarnating, opening and manifesting of your soul/resurrection and Goddess or God into your physical existence. It also activates and opens all protections on all levels and between them, and their merging and fusion.

This is a major completion and culmination. If all other work is finished, the opening will be instantaneous, though may seem slightly delayed in working through the levels from the top down, from Above to Below. This should open your Goddess or God Union, total union and your ascension fully and permanently. If it does not, the opening will happen as soon as possible, usually within three days, and no further requests will be needed. You must have completed all previous processes of *ESSENTIAL ENERGY BALANCING, ESSENTIAL ENERGY BALANCING II*, and this book. The processes and work from *RELIANCE ON THE LIGHT* are also highly recommended.

1. Ask to speak with Divine Director, your Goddess or God, and all of the Light.

2. Request the REPROGRAMMING AND REPATTERNING OF YOUR MULTI-COSMIC CREATION AND CREATION ON ALL LEVELS for the full, complete, perpetual, permanent and forever CONNECTION, INCARNATION, ACTIVATION AND OPENING of your soul, your Be-ing, your Goddess's or God's Be-ing, your union, total union, ascension and resurrection into your body and your life, along with all appropriate connection with the Light Above and Below, and total protection through all levels and systems, and between them.

3. Ask for the REPROGRAMMING AND REPATTERNING OF YOUR MULTI-COSMIC CREATION AND CREATION ON ALL LEVELS for the complete and appropriate MERGING, FUSION, TRANSFIGURATION, ACTIVATION, OPENING AND MANI-FESTING through all levels, all systems and between them for you, your Goddess or God, your union, total union, ascension, your resurrection and your soul, along with all appropriate connection with the Light Above and Below, and total protection through all levels, all systems, and between them.

4. Request DIVINE DISSOLUTION of all that prevents, delays or endangers any of the above and all of their origins and sources.

5. Ask to DESTROY AND OBLITERATE ALL BLUEPRINTS AND ENCODINGS ON ALL LEVELS AND THROUGH ALL SYS-TEMS THAT ARE NOT OF THE GLORY AND PERFECTION OF THE LIGHT.

6. Ask for CLEANSING, CLEARING AND PURIFICATION TO THE TOTALITY OF THE LIGHT.

7. Request ALL THAT IS NEEDED OF HEALING AND REGENER-ATION, REPLACEMENT, RE-CREATION, CONNECTION AND RECONNECTION, ACTIVATION, RESURRECTION, UNION AND OPENING; NEW ENCODINGS, BLUEPRINTS, DOWN-LOADINGS, PROCESSES, COMPONENTS, PROTECTIONS, PROGRAMMINGS, COMPUTERS AND SYSTEMS; AND ALL ELSE THAT MAY BE NEEDED, NAMED AND UNNAMED, KNOWN AND UNKNOWN, IN THE PERFECTION AND GLORY OF THE LIGHT.

8. Request DIVINE RENEWAL AND RESTORATION IN ALL THINGS, AND DIVINE GRACE AND ABSOLUTION AS NEEDED.

9. Ask for these healings for YOU, YOUR GODDESS OR GOD, YOUR UNION, TOTAL UNION, AND ASCENSION, FOR ALL

RESURRECTIONS OF THE LIGHT, ALL MEMBERS OF YOUR SOUL GROUP, FOR YOUR SOUL, and for all your connections with the Light, with the Earth, and with all that's Light in all Multi-Cosmic Systems.

10. Ask for these healings THROUGH ALL CONCENTRIC CIRCLES OF ALL REALITIES, INCLUDING BLISTER REALITIES, SIMULTANEOUS REALITIES, MULTIPLE REALITIES, ALL STATES OF EXISTENCE AND BETWEEN THEM, AND ALL OVERLAPS, INTERFACES, CONNECTIONS, AND BETWEEN THEM.

11. Request these healings through the PAST, PRESENT AND FUTURE, FOREVER AND NOW, IMMEDIATELY AND INSTANTLY, THROUGH ALL INFINITY AND ETERNITY, AND EVERYTHING IN BETWEEN.

12. Thank Divine Director, your Goddess or God, and all Be-ings of the Light.

Universal Healings

a) Make the request above for: ALL WHO ARE BRINGING IN THE GODDESSES AND GODS, all Goddesses and Gods of the Light, all Goddess/God Unions, total unions, ascensions, all resurrections of the Light, all souls and soul systems, and all members of the Light of all soul groups.

b) Repeat the request for ALL REALMS AND BE-INGS OF THE LIGHT, Above and Below, individually and collectively, as appropriate and needed for each.

c) Repeat the request for ALL UNIONS OF THE LIGHT of every type on every level and between them, and all components, connections, systems and souls thereof.

d) Make the request once more for ALL OF THE ALL.

Process XXII Absolute Divinity

THE CHAIN OF LIGHT BEGINS WITH THE LIGHT BEYOND AND PROGRESSES AS follows. The Light Beyond→ the Combined Ultimate Sources of the Light→ our Ultimate Source of the Light→ Multiple First Sources of the Light→ the First Source of our Multi-Cosmic system (First Mother, Eve)→ Multiple One Presences of the Light→ the One Presence of our Multi-Cosmos (Nada)→ all Presences of the Light (Kwan Yin and others)→ the Creator Light Ships and the technologies and Protectors of the Light (Angelic Realm)→ Our Great Cosmic Mother, The Overlighting Soul of the Above (The Shekinah and HaShem)→ the Differentiated Souls of the Below (Persephone, Aleyah, Nepthys, Aiyisha)→ the Goddesses and Gods of the Universe, Galaxy, Solar System, Moon and Earth→ all Be-ings and all life.

All souls and all of life are interconnected; we are one soul, the Soul of the Light. In the processes so far, we have cleared all souls as far as our Multi-Cosmic One Presence (Nada) from the Source of all Evil and all its creations and manifestations. There are many Cosmoses, therefore many One Presences. What next remains to clear is our Multi-Cosmic System's connections to our First Source, our First Mother Eve, and all of the Light beyond Her. Her domain is wider than is imaginable from our Earth viewpoint.

Kwan Yin, Goddess of healing and mercy, is Earth's liaison to First Mother. She is a Presence of the Light, on a level equal to The Shekinah. She accepts our requests and translates them, corrects them and makes them complete, to present them at the Multi-Cosmic System level and beyond. Some word process is required for this but much less than was required by Divine Director for requests within our Cosmos. Perhaps this is because we are unable to conceive of the intricacies involved, and therefore we are not asked to fully understand and comprehend, or to make our requests as detailed as they need to be. Our requests go to Kwan Yin, and She will take care of the rest. We are not to approach First Mother or the Absolute Divinities of Light beyond Her directly.

Use the following process for all that remains to trouble your life and life work, all that needs healed in you (and your soul and soul group), all that needs healed for your Goddess or God, Goddess/God Union, total union, ascension and resurrection, and all that needs healing and changing on Earth and throughout our (and all) Multi-Cosmic Systems and structures. By this time there should be very little left—most requests have been made and the healings and releases finished. For whatever does remain, however, this is your chance to go all the way to the top for resolution and healing. Do not hesitate to call upon Kwan Yin and to use this process for whatever you may need. All the karma that still remains will come up for healing now; use this process to release it and end it. Be sure to think very clearly about what it is that you want before phrasing your requests.

1. Ask to speak with Kwan Yin.

2. Ask Her to RESTORE THE MASTER PLAN AND THE PURE STATE OF ABSOLUTE DIVINITY OF THE LIGHT for your soul and for All of the All, and to put them into full perpetuality, effect and manifesting of the Light through all levels and all systems. This is for you, your Goddess or God, your union, total union, ascension, resurrection, for every member of your soul group, and for your entire soul and Multi-Cosmic System.

3. Request to END FOREVER, FROM ALL SOURCES AND ORIGINS, ALL RIPS, TEARS, HOLES AND BREACHES IN THE FABRICS OF BE-ING AND BE-INGS, including in your own Be-ing, and in all structures of all Multi-Cosmic Systems. Ask to REPLACE AND RESTORE IN ABSOLUTE PURITY AND PERFECTION ALL THAT IS MISSING, damaged, destroyed, undeveloped and improperly developed in your Be-ing and soul, and all blueprints, encodings, genetics and Master Plans of the Light involved. Request also to end all effects and results of these things

and to heal all damage and destruction for you, your Goddess or God, your union, total union, ascension, resurrection, for every member of your soul group, and for your entire soul and Multi-Cosmic System.

4. Ask in the name of Absolute Divinity and the Light for the HEAL-ING AND RELEASE OF ALL SUFFERING, DIFFICULTY, PAIN, DIS-EASE, AND KARMA that remain for you through all levels and all Multi-Cosmic Systems. This request is for you, your Goddess or God, your union, total union, ascension, resurrection, for every member of your soul group, and for your entire soul and Multi-Cosmic System.

5. Ask to RESTORE THE FULL CREATIONAL BIRTHRIGHT OF YOUR SOUL and every process, function, component, body and system of your soul and soul group in the Absolute Divinity of the Light through all Multi-Cosmic levels and systems. This includes every aspect of Be-ing and your Be-ing, including your joy, prosperity, union, perfect health and all Blessings of the Light for you, your Goddess or God, your union, total union, ascension, resurrection, for every member of your soul group, and for your entire soul and Multi-Cosmic System.

6. Request to END FOREVER—in every way that Absolute Divinity and the Light deem appropriate—THE SOURCE OF ALL EVIL AND ALL ITS CREATIONS, MANIFESTATIONS, EFFECTS, RESULTS, ALTERATIONS AND MUTATIONS, AND GENERATION OF DUALITY IN YOUR SOUL AND BE-ING, through all levels and all Multi-Cosmic Systems. Ask again for full restoration of Absolute Divinity's Master Plan and Pure State for your soul and Be-ing through all levels and systems. Ask that the Master Plan be put into full perpetuality, effect and manifesting of the Light of Absolute Divinity for you, your Goddess or God, your union, total union, ascension, resurrection, for every member of your soul group, and for your entire soul and Multi-Cosmic system.

7. Ask for all of these healings IN THE NAME OF ABSOLUTE DIVINITY AND THE LIGHT: Above and Below, individually and collectively, through all levels and all Multi-cosmic Systems, and amongst, amid, within, around, between, and through them. Request these healings for all Be-ing and Be-ings, all structures, and All of the All, as appropriate and needed for each.

8. Request these healings: THROUGH ALL CONCENTRIC CIR-CLES OF ALL REALITIES including blister realities, simultaneous realities, multiple realities, all domains and all states of existence.

9. Ask for them THROUGH ALL OVERLAPS, INTERFACES AND CONNECTIONS, and amongst, amid, within, around, between, and through them.

10. Ask for them through: PAST, PRESENT AND FUTURE, forever and now, immediately and instantly, through all infinity and eternity, everywhere, every when, everyone, everything, and all that is amongst, amid, within, around, between, and through.

11. Give thanks to Kwan Yin, to Absolute Divinity, and to the Light on all levels.

Universal Healings

a) Repeat the above requests and process for EVERY ASPECT OF EVERY SOUL AND BE-ING OF THE LIGHT, every Chain of Light, every structure, process, function, purpose, component, and Blessing of the Light through all levels and Multi-Cosmic Systems.

b) Ask for the above for ALL UNIONS OF THE LIGHT, all total unions, ascensions, resurrections, Great Goddess/God Unions, all connections, overlaps and interfaces involved, and all people manifesting all of these.

c) Ask for the above for ALL BE-INGS, all life, all the Light, all realms and species of the Light, and all people of the Light.

d) Request the above process for ALL STRUCTURES: Earth and all planets, our Moon and all Moons, our Solar System and all Solar Systems, our Galaxy and all Galaxies, our Universe and all universes, our Cosmos and all Cosmoses, all Multi-Cosmoses and Multi-Cosmic Systems, and beyond.

e) Make the above requests for all domains, grids, environments, belongings, energies, energy fields, and auras of the Light; all space, spaces and matter; ALL CREATION AND CREATIONS; all genetics; and all other aspects of creation and the Light through all levels and all Multi-Cosmic Systems, and beyond.

Process XXIII Transfiguring the Webs

THE FOLLOWING PROCESS ASKS FOR TRANSFIGURATION AGAINST ALL EVIL AT Absolute Divinity's Beyond Multi-Cosmic System levels, as well as for all other levels Above, Below and between. Where previous Transfiguring was of the levels and systems of your Creation and Be-ing, this process asks for Creational Repatterning, Reprogramming and Replacement to Transfigure not only your (and all) Creation but the raw materials and processes that creation and Be-ing are composed of. These raw materials include such energies as thought, word, voice, visualization, breath, intent, divine command, and the moment and propulsion of energy before each of these. It also includes such factors as genetics, Light, sound, vibration, frequency, energies of all types, space, spaces and matter, all creational processes, functions, programmings and computers, and all Creator Be-ings including Absolute Divinity, and beyond.

The following Transfiguration Against All Evil also includes the holograms, blueprints and Master Plans of First Mother's Creation of all Be-ings, and their projection and manifesting. We are holographic systems in which each cell, molecule and subatomic structure contains a copy of the wholeness and totality of our Be-ings. This means that the Master Plans of our Creational Birthright at Absolute Divinity's level is incorporated into every aspect, facet, process, component and function of our Creation and Be-ing on every level and through every Multi-Cosmic System. We are the microcosm (the smallest whole), and Absolute Divinity is the macrocosm (the greatest whole) of Be-ing. As Above, so Below.

Within us, the smallest facet in which the whole of Be-ing is carried is smaller than the smallest component of our known atomic structures. I have called these smallest components "particles." "First Particles" are the smallest and first creational components of life, Be-ing and Creation from which all other particles and aspects of Be-ing derive. They are both the sources and the end results of the holograms, and of the blueprints of our Creational Birthrights. In this case, we are the macrocosm/Above and these First Particles are the microcosm/Below of our Be-ings.

When the Webs of Life and Light—the hologram systems, projections, and the matrix of Particles and First Particles—are tightened and Transfigured Against All Evil and negativity, no evil or negativity in any form can ever again be created, nor can any evil or negativity previously created multiply, reproduce, regenerate or return. All evil and negativity that remains will be destroyed. We will be brought into Absolute Perfection and Absolutely Pure State in every aspect of our Be-ings, and only Absolute Light in its purity can penetrate, enter, exist or remain in our energies and Be-ings. Evil and negativity will no longer have effect, and can no longer Be. We have waited and struggled for a very long time for these protections and gifts.

Note that the Earth and all other structures also are comprised of these Webs.

1. Ask to speak with Kwan Yin. She is our liaison to Absolute Divinity and the Highest Light at Multi-cosmic and beyond Multi-cosmic levels. Do not approach First Mother or Absolute Divinity directly, but only through Kwan Yin's grace.

2. Ask in the name of Absolute Divinity and the Light for CRE-ATIONAL REPATTERNING, REPROGRAMMING AND REPLACE-MENT TO TIGHTEN AND TRANSFIGURE AGAINST ALL EVIL FOREVER THE WEBS AND HOLOGRAMS OF LIFE AND LIGHT in every aspect, projection, component, connection, process, function, symbol, manifestation, and creation of your soul and Be-ing through all levels and all Multi-Cosmic Systems and between them. This and all requests are for you, your Goddess or God, your union, total union, ascension, resurrection, your Great Goddess/God Union, for every member of your soul group, and for your soul. Request also, that all of the above, in Absolute Totality, be TRANSFIGURED FOR THE LIGHT FOREVER, AND UNTO THE LIGHT AND UNTO PROTECTION FOREVER.

3. Request that all of the above, and all of your soul and Be-ing in every aspect, component, body, connection and system, be brought to ABSOLUTE PERFECTION, ABSOLUTELY PURE STATE, ABSOLUTE PROTECTION, AND ABSOLUTE LIGHT in accordance with the Master Plans and holograms of Absolute Divinity and the Light on all levels and through all Multi-Cosmic Systems and between them, including all manifested and physical levels.

4. Request in the name of Absolute Divinity and the Light the ABSO-LUTE END OF THE SOURCE OF ALL EVIL AND ALL ITS CRE-ATIONS AND MANIFESTATIONS FOREVER, ALL THAT IT HAS CAUSED, AND ALL EVIL FOREVER, in all of its sources and ori-gins, Be-ings, creations and manifestations, repetitions, results and effects, Particles, First Particles, and holograms for you, your soul and soul group, and for All of the All.

    Ask for the ABSOLUTE DESTRUCTION, OBLITERATION AND END FOREVER OF ALL EVIL DUALITY, as well as all evil and negative mechanisms and symbols, all weaponry, harm, dam-age and destruction to the Light, all evil and negative science and technology, all evil and negative energies, sorcery, booby traps, triggers, trip-wires, activations of all types, remote activations, and all evil fail-safes of every kind and type.

    Ask for the ABSOLUTE DESTRUCTION, OBLITERATION AND END FOREVER OF ALL MULTIPLICATION AND REPLICATION OF EVIL AND NEGATIVITY in all forms, Particles and aspects, all exponential multiplication, all evil and negative alterations and mutations, evil and negative genetics, all duplication, generation, regeneration, reproduction, cloning, projection, and perpetuality of evil and negativity, and all misqualification of the Light.

    Request THE END FOREVER OF ALL NEGATIVITY AND EVIL—NAMED AND UNNAMED, KNOWN AND UNKNOWN—IN EVERY WAY THAT ABSOLUTE DIVINITY AND THE LIGHT DEEM APPROPRIATE, AND RESTORE TO ABSOLUTELY PURE

STATE ALL BE-ING AND BE-INGS, ALL STRUCTURES, AND ALL OF LIFE AND LIGHT IN ABSOLUTE TOTALITY.

5. Ask in the name of Absolute Divinity and the Light for CREATIONAL REPROGRAMMING, REPATTERNING AND REPLACEMENT TO RESTORE THE ABSOLUTELY PURE AND ABSOLUTELY PERFECT CREATIONAL BIRTHRIGHT OF YOUR CREATION AND SOUL, and of every Particle and First Particle, every blueprint, Master Plan, creational symbol, hologram and the projection thereof, and of every process, function, aspect, component, body, connection, manifesting and system of your soul and Be-ing, and between them.

6. MAKE THESE REQUESTS ALSO FOR ALL OF THE LIGHT, and all creations and manifestations of the Light, for every realm, species, Be-ing, aspect, process, creation and function, all structures and grids, all domains, environments, belongings, energies and energy fields, auras and auric fields, genetics, raw materials, Particles and First Particles, projections, holograms, creational symbols, computers, and for all souls and members of all soul groups, all of life and all that is not alive, all physical form and all forms, and all incarnations.

7. Request the ABSOLUTE PERPETUALITY OF THE ABSOLUTE PERFECTION AND ABSOLUTELY PURE STATE OF ALL WEBS OF LIFE AND LIGHT and all the requests above, in the name of Absolute Divinity and the Light.

8. Ask Kwan Yin to EXPAND ALL REQUESTS TO ABSOLUTE TOTALITY, ABSOLUTE COMPLETENESS, ABSOLUTE CORRECTNESS, ABSOLUTE PERFECTION AND ABSOLUTELY PURE STATE in all things, and to add all that has been missed to every request in the name of Absolute Divinity and the Light.

9. Request these healings IN THE NAME OF ABSOLUTE DIVINITY: Above and Below, individually and collectively, through all levels

and all Multi-Cosmic Systems, and amongst, amid, within, around, between, and through them. Request these healings for all Be-ing and Be-ings, all structures, and All of the All.

10. Ask for these healings: THROUGH ALL CONCENTRIC CIRCLES OF ALL REALITIES including blister realities, simultaneous realities, multiple realities, all states of existence, all lives and lifetimes including the present lifetime, all incarnation and reincarnation, and all of physical form.

11. Ask for these healings THROUGH ALL OVERLAPS, INTERFACES, CONNECTIONS, CORDS, COMPONENTS, SYSTEMS AND OVER-LIGHTING, and all that is amongst, amid, within, around, between, and through them.

12. Ask for them through: PAST, PRESENT AND FUTURE, forever and now, immediately and instantly, through all infinity and eternity, for everyone, everywhere, every when, and everything, and all that is amongst, amid, within, around, between, and through them, for All of the All, as appropriate and needed for each.

13. Give thanks to Kwan Yin, to First Mother, to Absolute Divinity, and to the Light on all levels.

Universal Healings

a) Repeat the above requests and process for every aspect of every soul and Be-ing of the Light, and for ALL CREATIONS AND MANIFESTATIONS of every member of all soul groups of the Light.

b) Repeat the above for ALL CHAINS AND WEBS OF LIGHT AND LIFE, all Continuity of the Light and Life, all Unity of the Light and Life, and all Blessings of the Light and Life.

c) Ask for the above for ALL UNIONS OF THE LIGHT, all total unions, ascensions, resurrections, Great Goddess/God Unions, and all who manifest them, as well as for their souls and every member of their soul groups, and all connections, overlaps, interfaces and over-lighting amongst, amid, within, around, between, and through them.

d) Ask for the above for ALL STRUCTURES: Earth and all planets, our Moon and all moons, our Solar System and all Solar Systems, our Galaxy and all Galaxies, our Universe and all Universes, our Cosmos and all Cosmoses, all Multi-Cosmoses and Multi-Cosmic Systems and beyond, and all that is amongst, amid, within, around, between, and through them.

e) Make the above requests for all domains, grids, environments, belongings, energies, energy fields, auras and auric fields of all of the Light; all space, spaces and matter; ALL CREATION AND CREATIONS; all computers; all genetics; and all other aspects of Creation and the Light through all levels and all Multi-Cosmic Systems and beyond, for All of the All, as appropriate and needed for each.

Process XXIV   Absolute Karmic Dissolution

THIS PROCESS IS TO CARRY ALL PREVIOUS REQUESTS FOR THE ENDING OF KARMA TO the ultimate level, that of the Combined Ultimate Sources of the Light and the master computer that is the Light Beyond. It will also serve to expand all other requests with regard to the ending of evil and negativity and their damage and effects for you and your Goddesses and Gods to the highest level. Those who complete ascension this far may find that instead of having a single Goddess or God to manifest through you, you may have a Family of Light of Goddesses and male divinities (Gods). They are members of your soul group who have now been resurrected. What I term Gods here may include members of the angelic realm (Angels, Archangels, Elohim), Presences of the Light, pure Twin Flames, ascended masters, saints or other male Light Be-ings. Male divinities are beginning to come in as Gods for men on the ascension path, in the way that Goddesses are and have been coming in for women.

1. Ask to speak with Divine Director, the Karmic Board, Kwan Yin, and First Mother. For this request, you are permitted to approach our First Mother directly.

2. Ask to make the following requests IN THE NAME OF THE COMBINED ULTIMATE SOURCES OF THE LIGHT, THE LIGHT BEYOND, and in your own name.

3. Request ABSOLUTE DIVINE DISSOLUTION FROM ALL KARMA WITH ALL EVIL AND NEGATIVITY of every kind and aspect, with all the effects and results of all evil and negativity, and with all evil and negative incidents and perpetrators.

4. Also request ABSOLUTE DIVINE DISSOLUTION FROM ALL KARMA of every kind and aspect, and from all the effects and results of all karma from all lifetimes, from all states of existence, and between them. (Only harm and suffering will be ended here, not karma you would wish to keep.)

5. Ask for ABSOLUTE DIVINE RESTORATION AND RENEWAL FOR ALL OF THE LIGHT with regard to the requests above.

6. Ask that these requests be EXPANDED TO ABSOLUTE TOTALITY, absolute completion, absolute perfection, and absolute correctness. Ask to add all else that may be needed, all that you have missed, and all that you don't know to these and all requests. Ask for all appropriate benefits and blessings of the Light.

7. Make these requests for yourself and for all others bringing in the Light, all Goddesses and Gods of the Light, all unions of the Light, total unions of the Light, ascensions of the Light, resurrections of the Light, Great Goddess/God Unions of the Light, and all souls and Be-ings of the Light.

8. Thank Divine Director, the Karmic Board, Kwan Yin, and First Mother. The granting of these requests is the Combined Ultimate Sources of the Light's (Absolute Divinities) gift for the protection and blessing of all who are bringing in the Light.

To Bring In a Goddess or God

If you have been chosen to bring your Goddess or God into your energy to fully manifest through you, you will know by now. Your Goddess or God will tell you, or Divine Director or the Karmic Board will make the information evident. Only women will bring in their Goddesses, though everyone has a Goddess and may be in contact with Her. Men will bring in male divinities, often Twin Flames of Goddesses, though only a few men are being chosen to do so as yet. Those who are chosen by their Goddesses or Gods have been selected for a variety of reasons. They are people on an ascension path, willing to do the work of clearing their karma, and of a Light level high enough to support Goddess/God energy merged with their own. Most are seriously doing some form of planetary service or service to people or animals; they may be healers, teachers, caretakers of animals or land, activists, or otherwise good role models for others and making a difference. They are people willing to devote their lives to the Goddess and their own Goddess or God, as well as to a path of service.

This is not a job for everyone, and while those suited for it will enjoy it tremendously, those not suited for it may find it more than they wish to complicate their lives with. Bringing in a Goddess or God will totally change your life, from under your skin to without. First of all, you will never be alone again, and you will never be unguided. Your choices and free will on many occasions will come second to your Goddess's or God's needs. You also may find that your Goddess or God needs a great deal of healing and has probably been under a great deal of attack. It will be up to you, with Divine Director, the Karmic Board and these processes, to heal Her/Him and to end the attacks on both of you. You will learn what She or He needs and how to make the requests. When She or He is merged with you, Her/His healing needs become your own, and if your Goddess or God is being attacked, you are being attacked as well.

The processes for clearing your karma and of the subsequent closing of your crown for reprogramming are not always easy or pleasant, and they are extended in those bringing in a Goddess or God. You must clear much more of your karma on all levels when bringing in a Goddess or God than you would need to for ascension without. You will also need to complete *Essential Energy Balancing* and *Essential Energy Balancing II* (*Reliance on the Light* is highly recommended), besides the processes of this book, and to complete the release of your karma through the Universe and Cosmos. All of this requires extended, dedicated, and often unpleasant work on your part, but if your Goddess or God chooses you and you complete the work, you will find it worth your while.

If you still wish to go further, and you have been invited by your Goddess or God to bring Her or Him in, the following is a summary of what is needed. Permission is required of the Lords of Karma, the Karmic Board, Divine Director and your Goddess or God for doing so. With that given, the following processes must be done, using the exact wording given below. If you receive a "no" to any request, ask what is needed to release the no and follow instructions, or ask to cancel all karma and all karmic contracts from Earth and all other planets, all lifetimes and between them, that may be the source of the no.

1. You must first complete all of the *Essential Energy Balancing I* and *II* processes, from my books *Essential Energy Balancing* and *Essential Energy Balancing II* (Crossing Press, 2000 and 2003). You must be working on the clearing of your Earth karma, or have completed it, and have the ability to make requests of the Lords of Karma and Divine Director. Your Energy Selves must be fully fused into your energy and your Light Body activated. If you have not already done these things, get the books and do them now.

You may be told at some point that you need to repeat some of the processes, do so.

2. Make the request of Divine Director, the Lords of Karma, and the Karmic Board to clear, heal, reconnect, and fully activate the full compliment of your DNA, if you haven't done so already. Only a "yes" is needed here, no process is required. You only need to do this once.

3. Request formally of Divine Director, the Lords of Karma, and the Karmic Board that you bring in your Goddess or God to fully merge with you and live with you on Earth. Ask for the name of the Goddess or God you will bring in. She or He is usually who was named as your Goddess or God in Essential Energy Balancing, but not always. Ask to cancel all karma and all karmic contracts from Earth and all other planets, from all lifetimes and between them, preventing you from bringing your Goddess for God in. (No process is required, only a "yes.")

4. Ask Divine Director, the Lords of Karma, and the Karmic Board to fully develop, establish, activate and open all Galactic Cord and Chain of Light components, systems and connections for you, your Goddess or God, your union, total union and ascension. Use Process XI of *Essential Energy Balancing II*, the Short Process, (given below), with the exact wording as follows. Use this process for all other karmic requests, as well; it is summarized again below.

SHORT PROCESS

Ask to speak with the Lords of Karma and Divine Director.

Make the request for you, your Goddess or God, your union, total union, and ascension, on Earth, all other planets and between them, through all lifetimes and between them, through all dimensions and multidimensions and between them, of and between all dimensions of your multidimensional Be-ing.

Ask for these things fully, completely, permanently and forever, through all the levels and components of your Be-ing, all dimensions, all connections, all systems, and between them, through all multidimensions and between them of and between all dimensions of you, your Goddess or God, your union, total union, and ascension's multidimensional Be-ing.

Ask for these things immediately and instantly, past, present and future, forever and NOW.

Thank Divine Director, the Lords of Karma, the Karmic Board, and your Goddess or God.

5. Request the full and complete healing of your Goddess or God, in accordance with the Light. Ask to cancel all karma and all karmic contracts from all planets, lifetimes and between them, through all dimensions, multidimensions and between them, that could prevent Her/His total healing. (No process is required here, only a "yes." Use the above precise wording. If you are shown what needs healing, use the Short Process to request that it be done.)

6. Ask to cancel *ALL* karma and *ALL* karmic contracts in totality from all lifetimes and incarnations on all planets and between them, including for this lifetime, for you, your Goddess or God, your union, total union, and ascension, past, present and future, forever and NOW. (No process is needed here, only a "yes.")

7. Do *Essential Energy Balancing II* Process XVIII—RE-CREATION AND REPLACEMENT (reprinted below).

8. Do Processes II and III from *Essential Energy Balancing III* (reprinted below). These are the SWORD, CHALICE, SHIELD FUSION, and INTERDIMENSIONAL SWORD, CHALICE AND SHIELD. They offer more complete protection for you and for your Goddess or God than you have received until now.

RE-CREATION AND REPLACEMENT

Your Creation is an energy component, a computer programming based upon and derived from the central programming of the planetary and beyond Mind Grid. Where there is significant energy damage, it is often easier for the Lords of Karma and Divine Director to replace a damaged component instead of repairing it or healing it. Planetary (and beyond planetary) damage replicates in the creation of all life. This process is to replace the damaged Mind Grid on all levels, as it manifests in your individual Creation.

NOTE: This process may result in the closing of your crown chakra for about a week as the reprogramming and replacements are made. You may feel periods of anxiety during this closing. If you have already done this work with *Essential Energy Balancing II*, this closing will probably not occur.

1. Ask Divine Director and the Lords of Karma to REPLACE AND RE-CREATE THE PROGRAMMING OF YOUR CREATION, deleting from it all attacks, damage, access, negative and evil programming, and negative and evil interference of all types by The Source of All Evil and all its creations and manifestations. Ask to delete also, all dis-ease, all that prevents your evolution and ascension, all that obstructs or prevents the full opening and function of your life purpose, all that keeps you from manifesting your full connection with the Light, and all that prevents the manifesting of your full Light and life force. (You may add to this list.)

2. Ask to REPLACE ALL COMPONENTS AND CONNECTIONS THROUGH ALL SYSTEMS THAT MANIFEST CREATIONAL DAMAGE OR EVIL AND TO RECONNECT ALL SYSTEMS TO ABSOLUTE PURITY AND PERFECTION, ABSOLUTE LIGHT AND LOVE.

3. Ask that The Source of All Evil, all its creations and manifestations, and the negatives and evils above be ANNIHILATED, EXTINGUISHED, UNCREATED AND OBLITERATED from your new Creation and energy through all systems.

4. Ask that your new Creation by programmed to CANCEL ALL KARMA AND ALL KARMIC CONTRACTS with the above deletions, with the Source of All Evil, and all its creations and manifestations.

5. Ask to HEAL AND REGENERATE ALL DAMAGE to your Creation and all systems, replacing all components and connections that are too damaged to easily heal. Ask for full reconnection of all energies, and for full and optimal function of all components, connections and systems. Ask for total safety and protection for your new Creation and all systems and connections forever.

6. Ask to TRANSFIGURE YOUR NEW CREATION against all the above deletions and The Source of All Evil in all of its creations and manifestations forever. Ask to TRANSFIGURE YOUR NEW CREATION FOR THE LIGHT FOREVER, AND UNTO THE LIGHT AND UNTO PROTECTION FOREVER. Ask to cancel all karma and all karmic contracts that prevent this total transfiguration.

7. Ask for all of these things in the name of the Light: through Earth and all other planets and between them, all lifetimes and between them, all dimensions and between them, through all multidimensions and between them, of and between all dimensions of your multidimensional Be-ing.

8. Ask for these things fully, completely, permanently and forever, through all the levels and components of your Be-ing, through all dimensions, all connections, all systems and between them, through all multidimensions and between them of your multidimensional Be-ing.

9. Ask for these healings immediately and instantly under Karmic Law, past, present and future, forever and NOW.

10. Thank Divine Director and the Lords of Karma.

Universal Healings

    a) Repeat the process above for ALL CREATION AND ALL LIFE.

    b) Make the same request for YOU, YOUR GODDESS OR GOD, YOUR UNION, TOTAL UNION, AND ASCENSION.

SWORD, CHALICE, SHIELD FUSION

In *Essential Energy Balancing II* (and in *Reliance on the Light*), you were given the Sword, Chalice and Shield of Archangel Michael. This time, these articles of protection are to be installed in your Creational Programming—for you, your Goddess or God, and your union with Her or Him. They are also to be installed in your total union, your ascension, and in your Galactic Cord and Grounding Cord systems, as well. The fusion, transfiguration and activation of these articles is the fusion, transfiguration and activation of your Goddess or God Union. As a number of protecting Archangels are now present for ascension candidates and their unions, I am replacing Archangel Michael's name with that of "your Dimensional Archangel" in the process. Your Dimensional Archangel may be Archangel Michael or another Archangel of the Light.

    1. Ask to speak with the Lords of Karma, Divine Director, your Dimensional Archangel and the Karmic Board. Request the REPROGRAMMING OF YOUR CREATION TO INSTALL YOUR DIMENSIONAL ARCHANGEL'S SWORD OF PROTECTION AND TRUTH IN YOUR ENERGY, YOUR GODDESS or GOD'S ENERGY, IN THE ENERGY OF YOUR UNION, IN YOUR TOTAL UNION AND ASCENSION, AND IN ALL GALACTIC CORD AND GROUNDING CORD SYSTEMS IN THEIR COMPLETELY SYNCHRONIZED AND COMPLEMENTARY STATE. The Sword's use is to fight evil and protect the Light. If at this step or any other of the process, your request is denied, ask what you must do to have it, and follow the directions that will be given to you. Otherwise continue.

2. If the request is granted, ask where the Sword is to be installed in each. There will be seven Swords, one in you, one in your Goddess or God, one in your union, one in your total union, one in your ascension, and one each in your Galactic Cord and Grounding Cord systems. They will be in seven different places. If the request is granted, but you are not shown locations, you may still continue.

3. Ask that the reprogramming be completed and the Swords be installed.

4. Now REQUEST THE REPROGRAMMING OF YOUR CREATION TO INSTALL YOUR DIMENSIONAL ARCHANGEL'S KARMIC SHIELD IN YOUR ENERGY, YOUR GODDESS OR GOD'S ENERGY, IN THE ENERGY OF YOUR UNION, IN YOUR TOTAL UNION AND ASCENSION, AND IN ALL GALACTIC CORD AND GROUNDING CORD SYSTEMS IN THEIR COMPLETELY SYNCHRONIZED AND COMPLEMENTARY STATE. The Shield protects you from the return of old karma.

5. If the request is granted, ask where the Shield is to be installed in each. There will be seven Shields, one in you, one in your Goddess or God, one in your union, one in your total union, one in your ascension, and one each in your Galactic Cord and Grounding Cord systems. They will be in seven different places. If the request is granted, but you are not shown locations, you may still continue.

6. Ask that the reprogramming be completed and the Shields be installed.

7. Next, REQUEST THE REPROGRAMMING OF YOUR CRE-ATION TO INSTALL YOUR DIMENSIONAL ARCHANGEL'S CHALICE OF HEALING AND REGENERATION IN YOUR ENERGY, YOUR GODDESS OR GOD'S ENERGY, IN THE ENERGY OF YOUR UNION, IN YOUR TOTAL UNION AND ASCENSION, AND IN ALL GALACTIC CORD AND GROUND-

ING CORD SYSTEMS IN THEIR COMPLETELY SYNCHRO-
NIZED AND COMPLEMENTARY STATE. The Chalice's use is for
the automatic self-healing of your energy.

8. If the request is granted, ask where the Chalice is to be installed
in each. There will be seven Chalices, one in you, one in your
Goddess or God, one in your union, one in your total union, one
in your ascension, and one each in your Galactic Cord and
Grounding Cord systems. They will be in seven different places.
If the request is granted, but you are not shown locations, you
may still continue.

9. Ask that the reprogramming be completed and the Chalices be
installed.

10. Now ask for THE FULL REPROGRAMMING OF YOUR CRE-
ATION FOR THE FULL, CONTINUOUS AND PERMANENT
ACTIVATION OF THE SWORDS, SHIELDS AND CHALICES IN
YOUR ENERGY, YOUR GODDESS'S OR GOD'S ENERGY, IN THE
ENERGY OF YOUR UNION, TOTAL UNION AND ASCENSION,
AND IN ALL GALACTIC CORD AND GROUNDING CORD SYS-
TEMS FOREVER. Request the complete insulation of your energy
to protect the full activations. Wait for this to be done; unless you
receive a "no" response, its happening. Ask when to go on.

11. Request the full activation of the Swords, Shields and Chalices.

12. When all seven Swords, Shields and Chalices in you, your
Goddess or God, your union, total union, ascension, and Galactic
Cord and Grounding Cord systems are fully activated, request the
following. Ask the Lords of Karma, Divine Director, the Karmic
Board and your Dimensional Archangel, for THE FULL REPRO-
GRAMMING OF YOUR CREATION TO MERGE AND FUSE,
AND TO TRANSFIGURE THE MERGING AND FUSION OF
THE SWORDS, CHALICES AND SHIELDS. The seven Swords
will be fused together, the seven Shields will be fused together,
and the seven Chalices will be fused together, thereby fusing you,

your Goddess or God and your union, total union and ascension into one. Ask when the fusion and transfiguration are complete; wait for this before going on.

13. Ask the Lords of Karma, Divine Director, the Karmic Board and your Dimensional Archangel for THE FULL REPROGRAMMING OF YOUR CREATION TO FULLY ACTIVATE THE FUSION AND TRANSFIGURATION OF THE SWORDS, SHIELDS AND CHAL-ICES, AND THEREBY FULLY ACTIVATE AND TRANSFIGURE YOUR UNION WITH YOUR GODDESS OR GOD. Wait for this to complete.

14. To finish, ask for these healings and reprogrammings in the name of the Light, on Earth and all other planets and between them, through all lifetimes and between them, through all dimensions, multidimensions and between them, of and between all dimensions of you and your Goddess's or God's multidimensional Be-ing, union, total union, and ascension.

15. Ask for these things fully, completely, permanently and forever, through all the levels and components of your Be-ing, all dimensions, all connections, all systems and between them, through all multidimensions and between them of you, your Goddess or God, your union, total union, and ascension's multidimensional Be-ing.

16. Request these healings and reprogrammings immediately and instantly, past, present and future, forever and NOW.

17. Thank the Lords of Karma, Divine Director, the Karmic Board, and your Dimensional Archangel.

Universal Healings

   a) Repeat the full process above, requesting it for ALL CRE-ATION AND ALL ENERGY.

   b) Do the full process above, wording it for the CREATION AND ENERGY OF YOUR GODDESS OR GOD, AND OF YOUR GODDESS OR GOD UNION.

c) Do the full process above, wording it for THE CRE-ATION AND ENERGY OF ALL THE GODDESSES AND GODS, GODDESS/GOD UNIONS, GREAT GOD-DESS/GOD UNIONS, AND ALL BE-INGS OF THE LIGHT.

d) Repeat the process again, wording it for THE CREATION AND ENERGY OF THE EARTH AND ALL PLANETS, ALL BE-INGS, AND ALL LIFE.

e) Repeat the process above, requesting THE REPROGRAM-MING OF YOUR CREATION AND ENERGY TO INSTALL YOUR DIMENSIONAL ARCHANGEL'S SWORD, SHIELD AND CHALICE IN YOUR HOME, GARDEN, CAR, COM-PUTER, BELONGINGS, PETS, AND CHILDREN. (Adults living in the home must make the requests for themselves.) Make sure the articles of protection are all installed and are fully and forever activated.

INTERDIMENSIONAL SWORD, CHALICE AND SHIELD

Your Interdimensional Archangel's Swords, Chalices and Shields protect you through the Galaxy's Interspace Grid, the spaces between the dimensions, where those of your Dimensional Archangel protect the dimensions of the Earth, Moon and Solar System. Added to your Dimensional Archangel's Swords, Chalices and Shields, those of your Interdimensional Archangel complete the total protections needed for the safety of your Goddess or God on Earth. Archangel Ashtar is the keeper of the Galaxy's Interspace Grid, but He is no longer the only Interdimensional protector for Goddess or God Unions. You may be given a different name for your Interdimensional Archangel.

You will note that as in the previous process there are seven Swords and Chalices. Here, however, there are eight (instead of seven) Shields. The additional Shield, the fusion of the combined protections, is provided by Archangel Metatron. It extends the protection and healing to and through the dimensions and interdimensions of our Universe.

1. Ask to speak with the Lords of Karma, Divine Director, your Dimensional Archangel, your Interdimensional Archangel, Metatron, and the Karmic Board. Request the REPROGRAM-MING OF YOUR CREATION TO INSTALL YOUR INTERDI-MENSIONAL ARCHANGEL'S SWORD OF PROTECTION AND TRUTH IN YOUR ENERGY, YOUR GODDESS'S OR GOD'S ENERGY, IN THE ENERGY OF YOUR UNION, IN YOUR TOTAL UNION AND ASCENSION, AND IN ALL GALACTIC CORD AND GROUNDING CORD SYSTEMS IN THEIR COMPLETELY SYNCHRONIZED AND COMPLEMENTARY STATE. The Sword's use is to fight evil between the dimensions. If at this step or any other of the process, your request is denied, ask what you must do to have it and follow the directions that will be given to you. Otherwise, continue.

2. If the request is granted, ask where the Sword is to be installed in each. There will be seven Swords, one in you, one in your Goddess or God, one in your union, one in your total union, one in your ascension, and one each in your Galactic Cord and Grounding Cord systems. They will be in seven different places. If the request is granted, but you are not shown locations, you may still continue.

3. Ask that the reprogramming be completed and the Swords be installed.

4. Now REQUEST THE REPROGRAMMING OF YOUR CREATION TO INSTALL YOUR INTERDIMENSIONAL ARCHANGEL'S KARMIC SHIELD IN YOUR ENERGY, YOUR GODDESS'S OR GOD'S ENERGY, IN THE ENERGY OF YOUR UNION, IN YOUR TOTAL UNION AND ASCENSION, AND IN ALL GALACTIC CORD AND GROUNDING CORD SYSTEMS IN THEIR COM-PLETELY SYNCHRONIZED AND COMPLEMENTARY STATE.

There is one further shield—that of Archangel Metatron's fusion of your combined Dimensional and Interdimensional protections—to make a total of eight levels. The Shield protects you from the return of old interplanetary karma.

5. If the request is granted, ask where the Shield is to be installed in each. There will be seven Shields, one in you, one in your Goddess or God, one in your union, one in your total union, one in your ascension, and one each in your Galactic Cord and Grounding Cord systems. If you see the eighth, it will be surrounding all the others at the end of this process. The seven Shields will be in seven different places. If the request is granted, but you are not shown locations, continue.

6. Ask that the reprogramming be completed and the Shields be installed.

7. Next, REQUEST THE REPROGRAMMING OF YOUR CREATION TO INSTALL YOUR INTERDIMENSIONAL ARCHANGEL'S CHALICE OF HEALING AND REGENERATION IN YOUR ENERGY, YOUR GODDESS OR GOD'S ENERGY, IN THE ENERGY OF YOUR UNION, IN YOUR TOTAL UNION AND ASCENSION, AND IN ALL GALACTIC CORD AND GROUNDING CORD SYSTEMS IN THEIR COMPLETELY SYNCHRONIZED AND COMPLEMENTARY STATE. The Chalice's use is for automatic self-healing in the spaces between dimensions.

8. If the request is granted, ask where the Chalice is to be installed in each. There will be seven Chalices, one in you, one in your Goddess or God, one in your union, one in your total union, one in your ascension, and one in your Galactic Cord and Grounding Cord systems. They will be in seven different places. If the request is granted, but you are not shown locations, you may still continue.

9. Ask that the reprogramming be completed and the Chalices be installed.

10. Now ask for THE FULL REPROGRAMMING OF YOUR CRE-
    ATION FOR THE FULL, CONTINUOUS AND PERMANENT
    ACTIVATION OF THE SWORDS, SHIELDS AND CHALICES IN
    YOUR ENERGY, YOUR GODDESS'S OR GOD'S ENERGY, IN
    THE ENERGY OF YOUR UNION, TOTAL UNION AND ASCEN-
    SION, AND IN ALL GALACTIC CORD AND GROUNDING
    CORD SYSTEMS FOREVER. Request the complete insulation of
    your energy to protect the full activations. Wait for this to be
    done; unless you receive a "no" response, it's happening. Ask
    when to go on.

11. Request the full activation of your Interdimensional Archangel's
    Swords, Shields and Chalices.

12. When all seven Swords, eight Shields and seven Chalices in you,
    your Goddess or God, your union, total union and ascension, and
    all Galactic Cord and Grounding Cord systems are fully activated,
    request the following. Ask the Lords of Karma, Divine Director, the
    Karmic Board, your Dimensional and Interdimensional
    Archangels, and Archangel Metatron for THE FULL REPRO-
    GRAMMING OF YOUR CREATION TO MERGE AND FUSE,
    AND TO TRANSFIGURE THE MERGING AND FUSION OF THE
    SWORDS, SHIELDS AND CHALICES. The seven Swords will be
    fused together, the eight Shields will be fused together, and the
    seven Chalices will be fused together. Ask when the fusion and
    transfiguration are complete; wait for this before going on.

13. Ask the Lords of Karma, Divine Director, the Karmic Board, your
    Dimensional and Interdimensional Archangels, and Archangel
    Metatron for the FULL REPROGRAMMING OF YOUR CRE-
    ATION TO FULLY ACTIVATE THE FUSION AND TRANSFIGU-
    RATION OF THE SWORDS, SHIELDS AND CHALICES, AND
    THEREBY FULLY ACTIVATE AND TRANSFIGURE THE INTER-
    DIMENSIONAL PROTECTION OF YOUR UNION WITH YOUR
    GODDESS OR GOD. Wait for this to complete.

14. Now ask the Lords of Karma, Divine Director, the Karmic Board, your Dimensional Archangel, Interdimensional Archangel, and Archangel Metatron for the FULL REPROGRAMMING OF YOUR CREATION TO MERGE AND FUSE, AND TO TRANSFIGURE THE MERGING AND FUSION OF YOUR INTERDIMENSIONAL ARCHANGEL'S SWORDS, SHIELDS AND CHALICES WITH THOSE OF YOUR DIMENSIONAL ARCHANGEL. Wait for this to be done; unless you receive a "no" response, it's happening. Ask when to go on.

15. Ask the Lords of Karma, Divine Director, the Karmic Board, your Dimensional and Interdimensional Archangels, and Archangel Metatron for the FULL REPROGRAMMING OF YOUR CREATION TO FULLY ACTIVATE THE FUSION AND TRANSFIGURATION OF THE COMBINED SWORDS, SHIELDS AND CHALICES OF YOUR INTERDIMENSIONAL AND DIMENSIONAL ARCH-ANGELS, AND THEREBY FULLY ACTIVATE AND TRANSFIGURE YOUR UNION WITH YOUR GODDESS OR GOD. Request also to FULLY ACTIVATE AND TRANSFIGURE THE TOTAL PROTEC-TION OF YOU, YOUR GODDESS OR GOD, YOUR UNION, TOTAL UNION AND ASCENSION, AND ALL GALACTIC CORD AND GROUNDING CORD SYSTEMS IN THEIR COMPLETELY SYNCHRONIZED AND COMPLEMENTARY STATE. Ask for the complete insulation of your energy to protect the full activation and transfiguration. Wait for this to complete.

16. To finish, ask for these healings and reprogrammings in the name of the Light, on Earth and all other planets and between them, through all lifetimes and between them, through all dimensions, multidimensions and between them, of and between all dimensions of you and your Goddess's or God's multidimensional Being, union, total union, and ascension.

17. Ask for these things fully, completely, permanently and forever, through all the levels and components of your Be-ing, all dimen-

sions, all connections, all systems and between them, through all multidimensions and between them, of you, your Goddess or God, your union, total union, and ascension's multidimensional Be-ing.

18. Request these healings and reprogrammings immediately and instantly, past, present and future, forever and NOW.

19. Thank the Lords of Karma, Divine Director, the Karmic Board, your Dimensional and Interdimensional Archangels, and Archangel Metatron.

Universal Healings

a) Repeat the full process above, but instead of doing it for your Creation and energy, do it for ALL CREATION AND ALL ENERGY.

b) Do the full process above, wording it for THE CREATION AND ENERGY OF YOUR GODDESS OR GOD, AND OF YOUR GODDESS/GOD UNION.

c) Do the full process above, wording it for THE CREATION AND ENERGY OF ALL THE GODDESSES AND GODS, GODDESS/GOD UNIONS, GREAT GODDESS/GOD UNIONS, AND ALL BE-INGS OF THE LIGHT.

d) Repeat the process again, wording it for THE CREATION AND ENERGY OF THE EARTH, MOON, SOLAR SYS-TEM, GALAXY, UNIVERSE, COSMOS AND BEYOND, ALL LIFE, ALL BE-INGS AND ALL THE LIGHT.

e) Do the full process again, wording it for THE CREATION AND ENERGY OF ALL PLANETARY GRIDS AND STRUC-TURES, INCLUDING THE WELL OF LIFE AND THE FIRE OF LIFE AT THE CENTER OF THE EARTH AND ALL PLANETS, AND THE PLANETARY CORE.

f) Repeat the process once more, requesting THE REPRO-GRAMMING OF YOUR CREATION AND ENERGY TO INSTALL YOUR INTERDIMENSIONAL ARCHANGEL'S

AND METATRON'S SWORD, SHIELD AND CHALICE IN
YOUR HOME, GARDEN, CAR, COMPUTER, BELONG-
INGS, PETS AND CHILDREN. (Adults living in the home
must make the requests for themselves.) Make sure the
articles of interspace protection are all installed and are
fully and forever activated.

These processes take twenty-four hours to complete, and you will feel it
happening. You will not be closed up for them.

If you have been given permission to bring in a Goddess or God, have
chosen and agreed to do so, and have done the work above, no more is
needed at this time. All requests from here on are for you, your Goddess
or God, your union, total union, and ascension. If you have not made
them in this way for the processes of this book, you may need to repeat
the processes. You will be told or know what needs healing in your
Goddess or God. To do these healings for Her or Him, make them as Short
Process requests for you, your Goddess or God, your union, total union
and ascension, unless you are told to vary this. You will be guided as to
what to do and what your Goddess or God needs, only follow the guidance of the Light.

Revised Daily Practice
Total Energy Clearing

This process is repeated from *Essential Energy Balancing II* as a general energy system clearing that should be repeated frequently—every night before sleep is optimal. Even after doing PROCESS IV—CREATIONAL ENERGY BALANCING in this book, you will find it helpful for the integration of all processes and requests. Ask for both the Lords of Karma and Divine Director with each step. Allow the clearing for each step to complete before going to the next. If at any step it feels as if the energy is stopped or not moving, ask what may be wrong. Is there a blockage or obstruction there? Is something disconnected, damaged, needing healing, repair or replacement? Ask for what is needed. Do you simply need to wait longer for the clearing to finish? Use this process as an all-energy diagnostic system as well as for all-energy clearing.

Since you have completed all the processes of *Essential Energy Balancing*, all of your Energy Selves are merged into your Goddess or God Self and your Goddess/God Self is merged into you. There is no need to call them in at the end of the energy clearing as you did in *Essential Energy Balancing*; they are already there. The steps of this process reflect your new energy components, developed since *Essential Energy Balancing* and *Essential Energy Balancing II*.

If you have not already done so, ask the Lords of Karma and Divine Director to clear, heal, reconnect and fully activate the full compliment of your DNA. All you need is a "yes" for this, no further process is required. This request is necessary for the work of

Essential Energy Balancing II and *III*, and you will not be able to bring in your Goddess or God without it.

1. Ask the Lords of Karma and Divine Director to clear, heal, align, open, activate, synchronize, fill with Light, repair, and reconnect your:

    ENTIRE TUBE OF LIGHT AND CRYSTAL SHAFT,

    and all chakras, chakra complexes, channels, connections and templates on all levels, all chakra systems, and all systems.

2. Ask the Lords of Karma and Divine Director to clear, heal, align, open, activate, synchronize, fill with Light, repair, and reconnect your:

    GROUNDING CORD ON ALL LEVELS TO THE CENTER OF THE EARTH AND BEYOND, INCLUDING ALL STRUCTURES, GRID STRUCTURES AND CONNECTIONS,

    and all chakras, chakra complexes, channels, connections and templates on all levels, all chakra systems, and all systems.

3. Ask the Lords of Karma and Divine Director to clear, heal, align, open, activate, synchronize, fill with Light, repair, and reconnect your:

    TEMPLATES ON ALL LEVELS,

    and all chakras, chakra complexes, channels, and connections on all levels, through all systems. List the following templates one by one, going to the next only after the previous template is cleared. Keep them in strict order.

    a) Ka template

    b) Etheric template

    c) Ketheric template

    d) Celestial template

    e) I-AM template

    f) All Galactic Body chakras and templates on all levels

    g) All Causal Body chakras and templates on all levels

    h) All Ascension chakras and templates on all levels.

4. Ask the Lords of Karma and Divine Director to clear, heal, align, open, activate, synchronize, fill with Light, repair, and reconnect your:

    HEART COMPLEX, HEART PANELS, AND ALL HEART SYSTEMS ON ALL LEVELS AND THROUGH ALL SYSTEMS,

    and all chakras, chakra complexes, channels, connections and templates through all of these, all chakra systems, and all systems.

5. Ask the Lords of Karma and Divine director to clear, heal, align, open, activate, synchronize, fill with Light, repair, and reconnect your:

    PHYSICAL AND ETHERIC BODIES,

    and all chakras, chakra complexes, channels, connections and templates on all levels, all chakra systems and all systems. List the following chakras one by one, going on only after the previous chakra is fully cleared.

    a) CROWN CHAKRA, chakra complex and chakra system on all levels, all systems

    b) THIRD EYE CHAKRA, chakra complex and chakra system on all levels, all systems

    c) THROAT CHAKRA, chakra complex and chakra system on all levels, all systems

    d) HEART CHAKRA, chakra complex and chakra system on all levels, all systems

    e) SOLAR PLEXUS CHAKRA, chakra complex and chakra system on all levels, all systems,

    f) BELLY CHAKRA, chakra complex and chakra system on all levels, all systems

    g) ROOT CHAKRA, chakra complex and chakra system on all levels, through all systems, to the center of the Earth and beyond, including all structures and grid structures.

6. Ask the Lords of Karma and Divine Director to clear, heal, align, open, activate, synchronize, fill with Light, repair, and reconnect your:

EMOTIONAL AND ASTRAL BODIES,

and all chakras, chakra complexes, channels, connections and templates on all levels, all chakra systems, and all systems. List the following chakras one by one, going on to the next only after the previous chakra is cleared. Keep them in order.

a) TRANSPERSONAL POINT CHAKRA, chakra complex and chakra system on all levels, all systems

b) VISION-CHAKRAS (2), chakra complex and chakra system on all levels, all systems

c) CAUSAL BODY CHAKRA, chakra complex and chakra system on all levels, all systems

d) THYMUS CHAKRA, chakra complex and chakra system on all levels, all systems

e) DIAPHRAGM CHAKRA, chakra complex and chakra system on all levels, all systems

f) HARA CHAKRA, chakra complex and chakra system on all levels, all systems

g) PERINEUM CHAKRA, chakra complex and chakra system on all levels, through all systems, to the center of the Earth and beyond, including all structures and grid structures

h) MOVEMENT CHAKRAS (2), chakra complex and chakra system on all levels, all systems, to the center of the Earth and beyond, including all structures and grid structures

i) GROUNDING CHAKRAS (2), chakra complex and chakra system on all levels, all systems, to the center of the Earth and beyond, including all structures and grid structures

j) EARTH CHAKRAS (2), chakra complex and chakra system on all levels, all systems, to the center of the Earth and beyond, including all structures and grid structures

7. Ask the Lords of Karma and Divine Director to clear, heal, align, open, activate, synchronize, fill with Light, repair, and reconnect your:

MENTAL BODY AND MIND GRID,

and all chakras, chakra complexes, channels, connections, and templates on all levels, all chakra systems, and all systems. List the following chakras one by one, going to the next only after the previous chakra is cleared. These chakras are not Kundalini (etheric body) chakras, but their mental body and Mind Grid counterparts.

    a) CROWN CHAKRA, crown complex, crown system on all levels, all systems

    b) THIRD EYE CHAKRA, third eye complex, third eye system on all levels, all systems

    c) LIGHT CHAKRAS (2), Light complex, Light system on all levels, all vision systems, all systems

    d) Chakras at the TOP OF THE THROAT, LIPS AND LOWER THROAT, AND ENTIRE THROAT COMPLEX, the throat system on all levels, and through all systems

    e) SOLAR PLEXUS CHAKRA, solar plexus complex, solar plexus system on all levels, all systems (Note: there is no heart or heart equivalent on the mental body or Mind Grid levels.)

    f) ROOT CHAKRA, root complex, all root systems, all systems, to the center of the Earth and beyond, through all structures and grid structures

    g) All chakras, chakra complexes, chakra systems on all levels and through all systems of the BREASTS, FINGERS AND TOES.

8. Ask the Lords of Karma and Divine Director to clear, heal, align, open, activate, synchronize, fill with Light, repair, and reconnect your:

SPIRITUAL, GALACTIC AND CAUSAL BODIES,

and all chakras, chakra complexes, channels, connections and templates on all levels, all chakra systems and all systems. The chakras for these are as follows, in sets rather than individually.

a) All chakras, chakra complexes, chakra systems on all levels and through all systems for the chakras of WILL, DESIRE, ATTAINMENT, ACTION AND PROPULSION, to the center of the Earth and beyond, through all structures and grid structures. (These are the galactic body chakras.)

b) All chakras, chakra complexes, chakra systems on all levels and through all systems for the chakras of SOUND, RECEPTION/INFORMATION, COMMUNICATION, MANIFESTATION, CREATION, AND IMPLEMENTATION. (These are the causal body chakras.)

c) The spiritual, galactic and causal body CROWN CHAKRA, crown complex, crown system on all levels and through all systems.

9. Ask the Lords of Karma and Divine Director to clear, heal, align, open, activate, synchronize, fill with Light, repair, and reconnect your:

ASCENSION AND RESURRECTION ON ALL LEVELS,

and all the chakras, chakra complexes, channels, connections, templates, and components of all ascension and resurrection processes through all systems. (Note: These processes operate through all the bodies. To request clearing for only the Ascension Body or Resurrection Body would be to limit the scope of this request for clearing.)

10. When the ascension and resurrection levels are fully cleared, the energy clearing is complete. Thank the Lords of Karma and Divine Director. This process is best done lying down at night before sleep. Follow it with an ESSENTIAL HEALING CIRCLE (*ESSENTIAL ENERGY BALANCING*—Process V) for a perfect night's sleep.

January 26, 2004
First Quarter Moon in Aries

Index